Scrapbooker's Alphabets

Stuv

B

Led

BOP

Scrapbooker's
Alphabets

INSPIRATION AND INSTRUCTION FOR
50 FABULOUS DECORATIVE ALPHABETS

Ruth Booth

A QUARTO BOOK

All inquiries should be addressed to:
Barron's Educational Series, Inc.
250 Wireless Boulevard
Hauppauge, NY 11788
www.barronseduc.com

Library of Congress Catalog Card Number: 2005934494

ISBN-10: 0-7641-3379-9
ISBN-13: 978-0-7641-3379-4

Conceived, designed, and produced by
Quarto Publishing plc
The Old Brewery
6 Blundell Street
London N7 9BH

QUAR: SBL

Editor: Michelle Pickering
Art editors: Claire Van Rhyn, Tania Field
Designers: Julie Joubinaux, Tania Field
Photographer: Martin Norris
Indexer: Dorothy Frame
Assistant art director: Penny Cobb

Art director: Moira Clinch
Publisher: Paul Carslake

Color separation by
Modern Age Repro House Ltd, Hong Kong
Printed by SNP Leefung Printer Ltd, China

9 8 7 6 5 4 3 2 1

CONTENTS

INTRODUCTION

This book offers instruction and inspiration for 50 hand-lettered alphabets in a wide variety of styles to assist scrapbooking enthusiasts who want their memory pages to be more personal and unique. The alphabets can also be used for other papercrafts, from writing invitations to greetings cards. The alphabet exemplars are sorted into categories for easy reference: Romantic, Playful, Funky, Exotic, Casual, and Classic. They include both lighthearted and formal letter styles, and can be used for titles, captions, or longer bodies of text.

Many of the alphabets are simple to learn and can be created using familiar tools, such as markers, graphite pencils, colored pencils, and gel pens. These alphabets offer solutions and options to the scrapbooker with limited time. Some alphabets offer more of a challenge to the crafter, giving the

opportunity to develop attainable skills and offering inspiration for unique alternate alphabets. There are also more demanding alphabets for those who enjoy calligraphy.

Each alphabet is displayed at actual size and includes a list of the writing tools that were used to create the model. A short introduction sets the mood for each alphabet and makes suggestions for appropriate applications. Helpful information is included about the construction, letter spacing, and the distinguishing features of each alphabet.

This is an excellent resource with clear examples and instructions that will give you the confidence to letter your memory pages in a way that is uniquely your own.

R Book

Each of the 50 alphabets is presented in the same clear format so that you can easily find the information required to re-create them in your own scrapbook pages.

HOW TO USE THIS BOOK

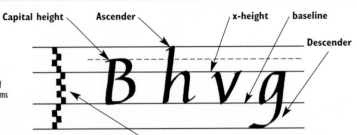

Capital height · **Ascender** · **x-height** · **baseline** · **Descender**

Terms
This illustration identifies the terms used to describe various elements of the alphabets. Refer to the glossary on pages 124–125 for concise definitions of these and all the other calligraphic and lettering terms used in this book.

Distinguishing features
Letter shapes within an alphabet need to share a number of characteristics in order to look like they belong together. The left-hand page of each alphabet includes a written description of the alphabet's shape, proportions, and characteristics, and is accompanied by three labeled examples to illustrate those features. Understanding the differences between the letter styles and the characteristics that relate the letters within an alphabet family is essential to good lettering.

Dominant pen angle
The dominant pen angle is the angle at which the pen is held most of the time for a calligraphic alphabet style (see also Pen-angle changes, opposite).

Letter height
The little black rectangles shown at the beginning of some alphabet exemplars are pen nib widths. These are used to determine the height of calligraphic letters (see page 11 for more information).

Introduction
A brief introduction to the alphabet, including ideas for applications.

Tools
The tools used to create the exemplar, plus alternative suggestions (see pages 13–15 for more information).

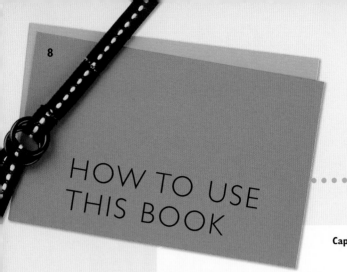

Guideline helpers
The fine lines at the right side of each exemplar are guideline helpers. They are designed to help you rule accurate guidelines quickly and easily in your own scrapbook pages (see page 10 for more information).

Note to scrapbookers
Cross-reference to matching upper- and lowercase alphabets, as appropriate.

Slant line
A slant line is shown at the beginning of an alphabet exemplar whenever an alphabet is written at a consistent forward slant. Slant lines have not been included for either upright alphabets or playful styles with letters that tilt forward and back.

Pen-angle changes

Pen angles are relevant only to alphabets made with a calligraphic tool. They refer to the angle of the broad edge of the pen tip relative to the baseline or writing line. Alphabets made with a pointed brush or monoline tool do not include this reference because those tools do not have a broad edge. The dominant angle at which the pen is held for a particular calligraphic alphabet style may need to be changed for certain letter strokes. This is indicated by a small box showing a different pen angle beside the relevant stroke. For instance, a slightly steeper pen angle is usually used to make the first and third diagonal in w so that the weight of those strokes is consistent with the weight of the downstroke in other letters. A very flat pen angle is used for the mid-stroke of the z so that it also has a weight similar to the downstroke of other letters in the alphabet family. Rotate the nib clockwise for steeper pen angles (45–60°) and slightly counterclockwise for flatter pen angles (20–0°).

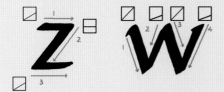

Letter-spacing guide

This shows the appropriate spacing between different types of letter shapes for each alphabet (see page 12 for more information).

Letter construction

Construction instructions for one or two letters are included with each alphabet. Step-by-step drawings are accompanied by written instructions to demonstrate how letter strokes fit together. Each step is shown in black, with any previous strokes shown in gray. Ductus arrows are included to show the direction of the strokes where appropriate. A small image of the tool tip is also included when the position of a calligraphy pen or brush is important. It may be helpful to look at the construction instructions shown for other alphabets made with the same writing tool; just be sure to follow the ductus and pen angle instructions included for the letter style you are doing.

Ductus

Gray arrows and numbers are shown beside each stroke of the letters on most alphabet exemplars. This is the ductus. Ductus lines are included whenever the direction and order of the strokes affects the construction of the letters. A certain stroke direction may be recommended because of the nature of the tool being used or because it makes it easier for writers to see what they are doing. Where there are ductus lines without numbers, the direction of the stroke is still important, but the letter is made with one continuous stroke. When drawing letter forms that have no ductus, you may find it helpful to rotate your writing page.

Variations

Some alphabets are easy to customize to the subject you are writing about, so a few ideas for alternate letter shapes are suggested as inspiration.

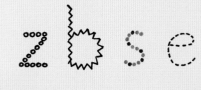

USING THE GUIDELINE HELPERS

Each alphabet exemplar has its own customized guideline helpers. When working at the same size as the alphabet exemplars, with the specified tools, use the guideline helpers to rule appropriate guidelines on your scrapbook pages.

1 Establish a reference line. Use the top of your page as a reference, or you can rule a line across your paper, just above the area where your guidelines will be.

2 Position the left side of your scrapbook page so that the top of the exemplar page is aligned with the top of your scrapbook page or with the reference line if you have drawn one.

3 Make a dot on your paper beside each line on the guideline helpers. Be sure that your paper does not move as you mark it. Repeat this process for the right side of your writing paper.

4 Using a ruler and an H or 2H pencil, connect the dots to draw guidelines on your scrapbook page. Keep the pencil lines light so that they will be easy to erase later.

COLOR CODING The guideline helpers are color coded to help you see at a glance which lines are which. The baseline is black; the x-height line is magenta; and the ascender/descender line is orange.

ADJUSTING THE LETTER HEIGHT

The relationship between the pen nib width and the letter height has a significant impact on the appearance of a calligraphic letter style, while monoline and drawn alphabets can be adapted to different sizes fairly easily, often with the same tool.

When lettering a calligraphic alphabet at a different size, you must use a different-sized broad-edged marker or pen nib. The x-height, descenders, and ascenders are measured in nib widths. An alphabet with an x-height of 4 nib widths will be smaller when written with a narrower nib and larger when written with a wider nib, but the alphabet's proportions will remain the same.

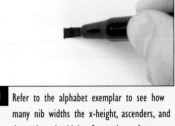

1 Refer to the alphabet exemplar to see how many nib widths the x-height, ascenders, and descenders should be. On a piece of scrap paper, draw a baseline. Position your pen or marker so that the width of the nib is at 90° to the baseline. Pull a short horizontal line along the baseline; it will look like a small box. In order to achieve accurate results, it is very important to position the pen nib accurately and pull short straight boxes at 90° to the baseline.

2 Maintain the 90° pen angle and make another little box, making sure that the bottom edge of this box aligns with the top edge of the previous box. Repeat this process until you have the correct number of nib widths, staggering the boxes so that you can identify how many there are.

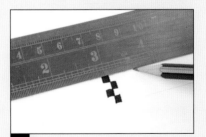

3 Once the ink is dry, rule a parallel guideline at the top of the staggered stack of nib widths. The distance between these two lines is your new x-height. Determine the ascender and descender heights using the same method.

MONOLINE AND DRAWN ALPHABETS

When adapting monoline and drawn alphabets to different sizes using the same tool, just be sure to maintain the same letter proportions. If the alphabet has ascenders and descenders that are the same length as its x-height, they should remain the same as the x-height when the lettering is done at a different size. A significant change in alphabet size may require a finer or thicker writing tool.

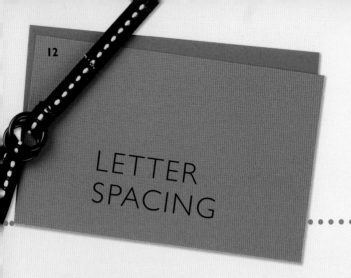

LETTER SPACING

Letter spacing creates texture on the page. Your lettering will be more pleasing, easier to read, and create a more attractive texture if it is spaced appropriately.

Letter-spacing guide

The letter-spacing guide has been designed to help you see the appropriate spaces between the letters more easily, while giving you a visual impression of a word written in each alphabet style. Alphabets with letters of consistent proportion and shape, such as Roman Majuscules (pages 108–109), need to be spaced evenly so that distracting dark areas or white holes are not created within the texture of the lettering. Uneven spacing is more appropriate for alphabets with inconsistent letter shapes and sizes, such as Child's Play (pages 44–45).

LOCVIR

ROMAN MAJUSCULES
Alphabets with consistent proportions and shapes require even spacing. The blue spacer equals the most difficult letter-spacing combination.

ILOEVRA

CHILD'S PLAY
Alphabets with inconsistent proportions and shapes can have uneven spacing.

Blue spacers

Alphabets that are more pleasing with consistent spacing have been assigned a standard-sized blue spacer. Lowercase alphabets, such as Ballerina (pages 20–21), have a spacer that is about the same size as the counter space in the n. Uppercase alphabets with letters of classic proportions are given a spacer about equal to the most difficult letter-spacing combination.

iloevra

BALLERINA
Consistent lowercase alphabets have a spacer equal to the counter space in the n.

For instance, in Roman Majuscules, the LA combination presents a challenge because even when those two letters are tucked closely together, there is still a significant space. The standard spacer varies from one alphabet to another because letter shapes and weights vary. Block letters—an alphabet with letters that are all about the same width, such as Art Deco Capitals (pages 58–59)—are simply placed side by side.

LOCVIR

ART DECO CAPITALS
Block letters should simply be placed side by side.

Letter types

The letters featured in the letter-spacing guide have been chosen to demonstrate the relationships between a variety of letter types: straight-sided letters (il), straight and round (lo), round and round (oe), open and diagonal (ev), diagonal and straight (vr), open and round or open (ra). In order to achieve letter spacing that looks reasonably consistent, we need to determine visually where the letter ends and the space between the letters begins. Our eye tends to borrow a portion of the area around and within some letters and add it to the space between the letters. That is why the blue spacer boxes sometimes overlap a portion of the letters.

WRITING TOOLS

The writing tools used to create the alphabet exemplars in this book are commonly found in most art and craft stores. Some of them have even been developed and manufactured specifically for scrapbooking.

Graphite pencil

A common monoline tool with a graphite writing tip that can be sharpened to a point or used dull and rounded. Pencils are graded on a scale from H (hardness) to B (blackness). Very hard pencils (9H) lay down little graphite and are therefore lighter on the page, but may score the paper. Very soft pencils (9B) lay down more graphite and are therefore darker on the page, but smudge easily. HB indicates the middle of the range. Artist-quality graphite pencils are archival.

Colored pencil

A monoline tool that can be sharpened to a point or used rounded and dull; available in a range of qualities. Artist-quality offers the richest, most permanent, and lightfast color.

Soft white eraser

Soft, so that it will not damage the paper; white, so that it will not leave a colored residue.

Crayon

Children's nontoxic wax crayons are not considered archival or lightfast.

Ballpoint pen

Common monoline writing tool with its own ink cartridge. The ink in these pens is not lightfast unless indicated on the label.

Gel pen
A monoline tool that comes in a wide variety of colors and qualities. Some are permanent and acid-free.

Colored fine-line marker
A fine-tipped monoline tool that comes in a wide range of colors. These markers are not permanent or archival unless indicated on the label.

Pigmented fine-line marker
Monoline tool that comes in a range of fine tips. The rendered line width is shown in millimeters on the label. Most brands are permanent and archival.

Medium-point permanent marker
A monoline tool with a slightly larger tip than the fine-line markers. These are waterproof and lightfast, but may not be acid-free. Note that these markers also come in a variety of colors, but that not all colors are permanent.

Double-ended permanent marker
Two monoline tools in one: a fine tip at one end and a broad tip at the other. Several brands developed specifically for scrapbooking have pigmented ink and are archival.

Modified popsicle stick
A flat wooden stick about ⅜ inch (10 mm) wide, with one end cut off and sanded smooth. It is used with an ink pad to stamp Stick Letters (pages 70–71).

Modified tongue depressor
A flat wooden stick about ½ inch (13 mm) wide, with one end cut off and sanded smooth. It is used with an ink pad to stamp Stick Letter Capitals (pages 72–73).

Ink pad
Available in a wide range of colors for rubber stamping. Many are pigmented and archival.

Ink

Use carbon-based or pigmented ink. Avoid India ink and inks that have shellac in them because they may remain sticky.

Pigmented calligraphy marker

A marker with a broad-edged tip. There are several archival brands developed specifically for scrapbooking. These come in a range of tip widths labeled in millimeters.

Calligraphy fountain pen

A tool with interchangeable broad-edged tips of different sizes and its own reservoir of ink. The ink in these pens is not lightfast or waterproof.

Broad-edged dip pen

Metal broad-edged nibs that fit into a handle. These come in a range of sizes and require a separate ink source.

Fiber-tipped brush marker

Comes in a range of sizes with a flexible tip that imitates the shape of a pointed brush. Some brands are archival and have pigmented ink, but note that not all colors are permanent.

Pointed brush pen

This is a pen because it has its own ink cartridge; it is also a brush because it has a real pointed brush tip. It comes in a variety of colors, but it is not permanent or lightfast.

LONGEVITY Crafters who want their scrapbooks to last for generations should use papers, writing fluids, adhesives, and embellishments that are pH neutral, lignin-free, and lightfast. Items that are waterproof and/or acid-free are not necessarily archival. A waterproof marker will repel water but may not be lightfast. Acid-free does not always mean pH neutral, and items that are very alkaline are no more archival than ones that are very acidic. Some writing media not labeled archival is still reasonably safe and long lasting. If archival scrapbooking is important to you, please take time to research the products available.

ALTERNATIVE TOOLS The alphabet exemplars in this book are shown at actual size. Each alphabet includes a list of the tools used to create the exemplar. If you use the writing tools listed, letter at the size shown, and follow the instructions, you can achieve similar results. A list of alternative tools is also included with each alphabet. Often the alternative tools are readily available and just as easy to use as those used to create the exemplar, although the calligraphic alternatives may be more difficult for a novice user. If you use an alternative tool, the results may still be pleasing, but they will differ from the model.

GETTING STARTED

There are some simple things you can do to ensure a more comfortable and successful lettering experience.

Slanted surface

Use a slanted work surface or lapboard to help avoid back strain. A flat, sturdy board about 18 x 24 inches (45 x 60 cm) will work well. Sit in a chair at a table with your back straight. Rest one end of the board in your lap and lean it against the edge of the table. Adjust the angle of the board by moving your chair closer to or farther from the table.

Good lighting

Work in a well-lit area. Good lighting will limit eyestrain and help you to work more accurately. Natural light is best, but bright light from an overhead source is also very helpful.

Padding

Work on a padded surface. Tape several layers of clean scrap paper to your lapboard or work surface. This padding helps ensure that you do not transfer unwanted textures from your work surface to your lettering. It also compensates for slightly uneven pressure when working with a calligraphy pen or stamped images.

Protect your paper

The moisture and oils from your hand may leave a residue on your paper that will repel writing fluid. To protect the paper, you can either keep a piece of scrap paper under your hand as you write or wear a hand guard. To make a hand guard, simply cut the ribbed end off an old sock and snip a small thumb hole in it about an inch or so (2.5 cm) from the end. Wear the hand guard on your writing hand whenever you are lettering.

Test your tools

Always have an extra piece of the same paper you will be working on so that you can test your writing tools. Markers will bleed on some papers, and certain colors will not show up very well on dark or brightly colored background papers. Check that the writing tip on markers has not become soft or mushy and replace the marker if it has lost its fine edge.

Do a rough draft

It is always advisable to write out your wording on a piece of scrap paper, at the same size and with the writing tool you intend to use for your finished work. Ensure that the placement, spacing, size, and layout will work before you begin writing on the finished page. Practice more complicated letter forms over a period of time before using them in your scrapbooks.

Explore your options

Sometimes a little "playtime" pays off. Try a variety of page layouts. Consider writing on a different art paper, tear around your lettering, and adhere that to your scrapbook pages. Experiment with other lettering styles, or try using a different writing tool or a different colored pencil or marker.

Use guidelines—most of the time

Even a very experienced calligrapher uses guidelines. Take the time to ensure that your lines are straight and parallel to the top and bottom of your page. The guideline helpers are useful when you are lettering at the same size shown on the exemplar (see page 10). Rule them very lightly with an H or 2H pencil so that they can be erased easily. There are some letter styles that may not require a full set of guidelines. If you choose to use your own handwriting or a very loose style such as Child's Play (pages 44–45), a simple baseline is fine.

L M N O P

G H I J K L

W X Y Z

R S T U V

ABCDEF

LETTERING STYLES

This section features 50 unique hand-lettered alphabets. Each alphabet is presented in the same clear format, with technical information on the left-hand page and the finished exemplar on the right-hand page. They have been organized into six categories that reflect the general mood of the alphabets—Romantic, Playful, Funky, Exotic, Casual, and Classic—to help you find an alphabet suitable for your subject, but your final choice will be a matter of personal taste. Use these alphabets exactly as they appear, or adapt them to suit your own purposes; above all, have fun creating memorable scrapbook pages and other papercrafts.

FGHIJK

BALLERINA

This tall, graceful alphabet has a formal appeal that is ideal for recording the special occasions in a young woman's journey through life. The main bodies of the letters are carefully written with a calligraphy fountain pen, and delicate serifs are added with a fine-line marker. To create the letters in a different size, remember to use two markers with different-sized tips to maintain the relative proportions of the letters and serifs.

NOTE TO SCRAPBOOKERS Adapt Italic Capitals (pages 106–107) to use as uppercase letters for Ballerina.

TOOLS
1.5 mm calligraphy fountain pen
0.35 mm pigmented fine-line marker

Alternative tools:
Use a calligraphy marker or broad-edged dip pen in place of the fountain pen.

DISTINGUISHING FEATURES

Ballerina is based on italic letter shapes, but has an unusually tall x-height. This alphabet is written with a dominant pen angle of about 35°. Letters branch at mid x-height and have angular bowls that are consistent in size and shape. The descenders are 8 nib widths long, slightly more than the ascenders, which are 7 nib widths long. Delicate serifs are accented with tiny balls at either end. The f, l, r, t, and x are reminiscent of a ballerina on her toes where the pen angle is revealed when the serifs are drawn parallel to the baseline.

Crossbar hangs just under the guideline

8° letter slant

Serif drawn parallel to the baseline reveals "ballerina" pen angle

LETTER-SPACING GUIDE

All letters sit on the baseline. See page 12 for more information on letter spacing.

iloevra

Ascender is 7 nib widths long

Mid x-height branching

x-height is 12 nib widths high

Angular bowl

Serif has a small ball at each end

Descender is 8 nib widths long

LETTER CONSTRUCTION: A

1 Holding the fountain pen at a 35° angle, pull slightly left, drop down toward the baseline, and then bounce up almost to the top of the x-height.

2 Maintaining a 35° pen angle, add the top of the bowl with the second stroke.

3 Close the bowl with the third stroke, again with the pen at a 35° angle. Note that the letter is at an 8° slant.

4 Add serifs with weighted ends using a fine-line marker.

LETTER CONSTRUCTION: W

1 Hold the fountain pen at a 45° angle to draw the first stroke.

2 Flatten the pen angle to 30° for the second stroke.

3 Steepen the pen angle to 45° again for the third stroke.

4 Flatten the pen angle back to 30° for the fourth stroke.

5 Use a fine-line marker to add a weighted serif.

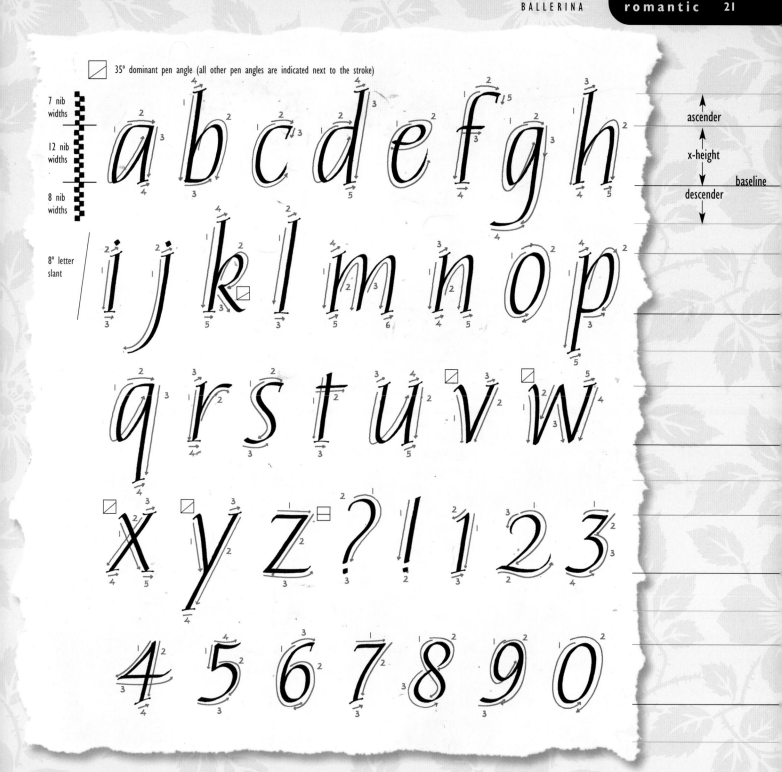

35° dominant pen angle (all other pen angles are indicated next to the stroke)

7 nib widths

12 nib widths

8 nib widths

8° letter slant

ascender

x-height

baseline

descender

ISABELLA

Inspired by a traditional handwritten script, this alphabet has elegant proportions and a gentle rhythm that make it ideal for greeting cards, picture labels, and captions about afternoon tea parties, romantic weekends, or church gatherings. Long bodies of text will need a lot of space due to the very long ascenders and descenders. A variety of letter sizes can be achieved using the same writing tool.

NOTE TO SCRAPBOOKERS Use Isabella Capitals (pages 24–25) as the uppercase letters for this alphabet.

TOOLS 0.35 mm pigmented fine-line marker

Alternative tools: Pencil, colored pencil, or colored fine-line marker

DISTINGUISHING FEATURES

This letter style is written at an extreme slant of 38°. Subtle shading is added to the r, the shortened descender of the p, and the elongated t. This provides contrast and helps relate the lowercase letters to the elaborately shaded capitals. Additional interest is created by the unusual crossbar that hovers above the t. These letters are written rhythmically as a continuous script, with looped ascenders and descenders that are almost three times the length of the x-height and consistently shaped oval bowls.

Oval bowl

Lead-in stroke

Looped descender is almost three times as long as the x-height

LETTER-SPACING GUIDE

All letters sit on the baseline. See page 12 for more information on letter spacing.

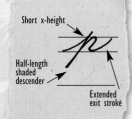

iloevra

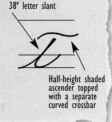

Short x-height

Half-length shaded descender

Extended exit stroke

38° letter slant

Half-height shaded ascender topped with a separate curved crossbar

LETTER CONSTRUCTION: M

1 Begin with the lead-in portion of the letter. Note that the letter is on a 38° slant.

2 Retrace until about halfway up the x-height and then branch out to make the first counter space.

3 Retrace halfway up the x-height again and then branch out to make the second counter space. End with the exit stroke.

LETTER CONSTRUCTION: D

1 Begin with the lead-in portion of the letter. Note that the letter is on a 38° slant.

2 Continue by drawing the bowl.

3 Continue up the ascender and outline the shaded top. Retrace and extend the ascender down to the baseline. End with the exit stroke.

4 Fill in the shaded top of the ascender.

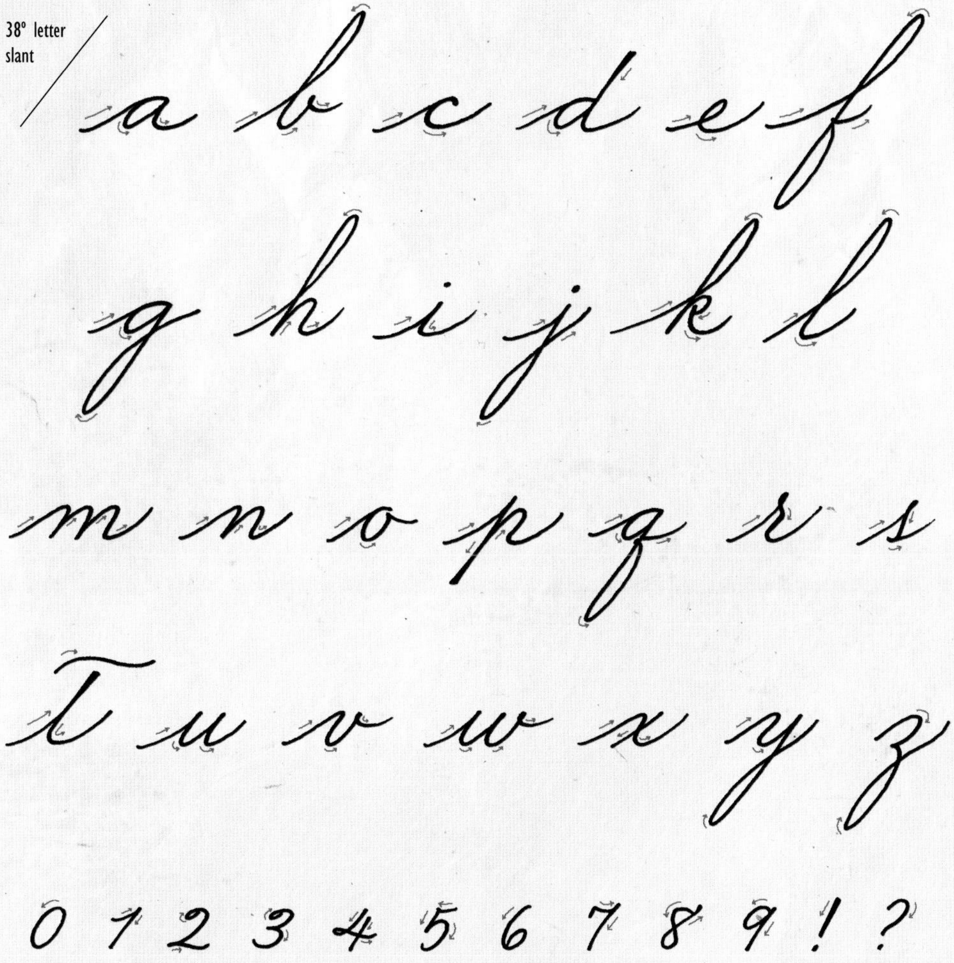

38° letter
slant

/ a b c d e f

g h i j k l

m n o p q r s

T u v w x y z

0 1 2 3 4 5 6 7 8 9 ! ?

ascender
x-height   baseline
descender

ISABELLA CAPITALS

These elaborate letters were inspired by an alphabet traditionally written with a flexible-pointed dip pen. Shading is outlined and filled in where the penman would have added pressure to the pen nib to widen the stroke. Due to its extensive flourishing, only use these capital letters with the lowercase Isabella alphabet rather than alone. This alphabet can easily be adapted to larger lettering without changing the writing tool.

NOTE TO SCRAPBOOKERS Use Isabella (pages 22–23) as the lowercase letters and numbers for this alphabet.

TOOLS
0.35 mm pigmented fine-line marker

Alternative tools:
Pencil, colored pencil, or colored fine-line marker

DISTINGUISHING FEATURES

These large capitals have consistently shaped oval bowls that are echoed by elaborate oval flourishes. Carefully drawn shading accents each of these extravagant letters. All of the letters are drawn fluidly with a long, continuous motion and at an extreme slant of 38°. The exit strokes need to be adjusted to accommodate the lowercase letters that follow them. Practice is needed to draw these capitals consistently.

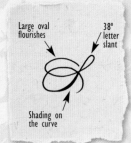

Large oval flourishes

38° letter slant

Shading on the curve

LETTER-SPACING GUIDE

This uppercase alphabet was designed for use only with the lowercase letters, not to be used alone. These three spacing examples demonstrate some upper- and lowercase letters together.

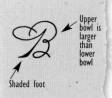

See page 12 for more information on letter spacing.

Upper bowl is larger than lower bowl

Shaded foot

Curves sometimes break through guidelines

Oval counter space

LETTER CONSTRUCTION: P

1 Begin the flourish below the top guideline, then complete the first stroke by outlining a small area for shading.

2 Begin the second stroke well within the flourish. Note that the bowl is oval.

3 Carefully fill in the shaded foot.

LETTER CONSTRUCTION: F

1 Begin the flourish below the top guideline, then complete the first stroke by outlining a small area for shading.

2 Begin the second stroke in the center of the flourish.

3 Add a small crossbar.

4 Carefully fill in the shaded foot.

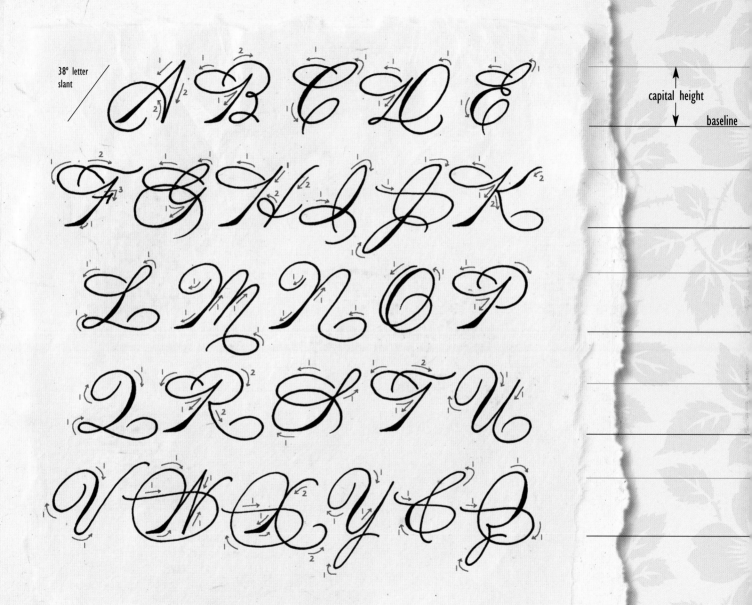

38° letter slant

capital height

baseline

ROMEO

Majestic letter proportions made with a humble writing tool give this alphabet a gentle but honorable appearance. These letters need to be drawn slowly and carefully. Romeo is a fitting alphabet for love poems or captions about your loved one, helping you to create scrapbook pages that proclaim your dreams. It is an alphabet you can linger over once those dreams have come true. Use the same tool to draw the letters in a range of sizes.

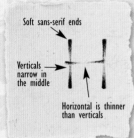

NOTE TO SCRAPBOOKERS
Romeo does not require a coordinating lowercase alphabet.

TOOLS
6B pencil

Alternative tools:
Colored pencils

Distinguishing features

Each stroke is carefully built up by retracing it several times. Use a pressure–release–pressure technique to create strokes with thinner, lighter midsections. This alphabet has classic proportions and includes signature O and M shapes. Pencil gives the letters a lovely soft texture. The graphite is likely to smudge, so you may want to create this effect purposely using a finger or stub of paper.

Strokes built up by multiple retracing

Bowl weight sits above center

Classic letter proportions

LETTER-SPACING GUIDE

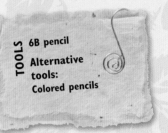

LOCVIR

All letters sit on the baseline. See page 12 for more information on letter spacing.

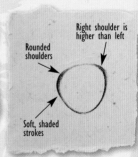

Soft sans-serif ends

Verticals narrow in the middle

Horizontal is thinner than verticals

Right shoulder is higher than left

Rounded shoulders

Soft, shaded strokes

LETTER CONSTRUCTION: M

1 Using a dull 6B pencil, draw the first stroke so that it leans slightly forward, adding pressure at the start and end, and releasing pressure in the middle.

2 Begin the second stroke with pressure, release, then add pressure as you approach the curve. Release on the way back up. The curve is off-center and does not meet the baseline.

3 Begin the third stroke with pressure, release, then add pressure again toward the bottom. Note that this stroke leans slightly backward.

4 Retrace the letter using pressure–release–pressure strokes until the letter is as substantial as you want it to be.

LETTER CONSTRUCTION: R

1 Using a dull 6B pencil, draw the first stroke, applying pressure at the start and end, and releasing pressure in the middle.

2 Begin the bowl stroke with pressure, release, then add pressure again as you round the curve. Release as you complete the curve. The bowl ends just below center height.

3 Begin the leg stroke using pressure, release for the midsection, then add pressure toward the end.

4 Retrace the letter using pressure–release–pressure strokes until the letter is as substantial as you want it to be.

capital height

baseline

ART NOUVEAU

These slightly unusual, Art Nouveau-inspired letter forms incorporate small oval curls to produce a simple, sweet little alphabet that is easy to use. It is suitable for titles and text about childhood romances or lovable but quirky old friends, or for humorous captions to accompany photos of children dressed up in Grandma's bonnet and high heels. This alphabet can be written at a range of x-heights using the same monoline tool.

NOTE TO SCRAPBOOKERS Use Art Nouveau Capitals (pages 30–31) as the uppercase letters for this alphabet.

TOOLS 0.50 mm pigmented fine-line marker

Alternative tools: Any monoline writing tool

DISTINGUISHING FEATURES

These vertical, high-branching letters have short serifs and oval bowls. The signature feature of the alphabet is the oval curls, which are also found in the accompanying uppercase alphabet. Each letter includes an oval curl, either within the body or as a foot. Take special note of the angle of the oval-curl feet. The body of these letters sits comfortably under the high waist of the uppercase letters, and the ascenders and descenders are slightly shorter than the x-height.

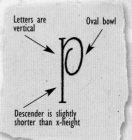

Letters are vertical

Oval bowl

Descender is slightly shorter than x-height

LETTER-SPACING GUIDE

All letters sit on the baseline. See page 12 for more information on letter spacing.

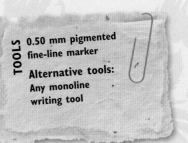

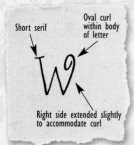

Short serif

Oval curl within body of letter

Right side extended slightly to accommodate curl

High branching

Ascender is slightly shorter than x-height

Oval-curl foot

LETTER CONSTRUCTION: M

1 Beginning at the top, draw a vertical stroke.

2 Start the second stroke about mid x-height within the first stroke, tracing the first stroke briefly before branching out.

3 Begin the third stroke so that it overlaps the second, making the counter space as wide as the first one at the top, then narrowing it toward the bottom to make room for the curled foot.

4 Add a short serif to the top and bottom of the first stroke.

LETTER CONSTRUCTION: V

1 Beginning at the top, draw a diagonal stroke.

2 Start the second stroke with an oval curl at the top. The curl should break the guideline.

3 Add a short serif to the top of the first stroke.

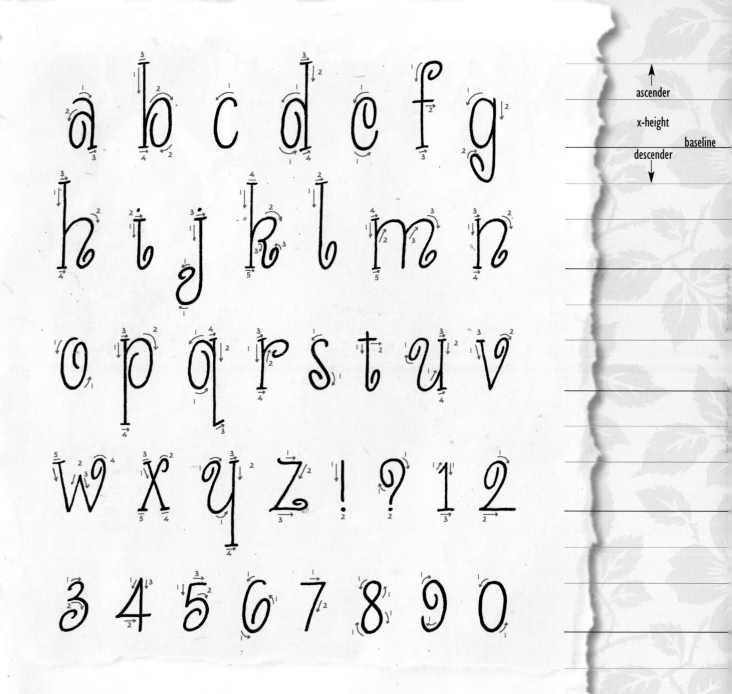

ascender
x-height
baseline
descender

ART NOUVEAU CAPITALS

Inspired by chic Art Nouveau styling, this alphabet has a few eccentric but endearing twists. The letters can be used alone for titles or captions, or with lowercase Art Nouveau for longer bodies of text. The tall, elegant letters have just the right humorous touch for writing romantic comedy stories. The same tools can be used to draw the letters slightly taller; for shorter letters, use a narrower calligraphy marker.

NOTE TO SCRAPBOOKERS Use Art Nouveau (pages 28–29) as the lowercase letters and numbers for this alphabet.

TOOLS
2.0 mm pigmented calligraphy marker
0.50 mm pigmented fine-line marker

Alternative tools:
Use a broad-edged dip pen or calligraphy fountain pen in place of the calligraphy marker.

DISTINGUISHING FEATURES

These letters are vertical, fairly narrow, and consistent in height. They are high waisted and slightly wider at the top than the bottom, with oval-shaped curls of various sizes incorporated into each letter. There is a signature oval-curl foot, reminiscent of old-fashioned iron patio furniture, on the A, K, M, and R, and large oval curls within many of the other letter forms. Those oval curls are echoed by the curled serifs that adorn the double-stroked verticals. The consistency of the double-stroked verticals lends stability and elegance to these otherwise offbeat letter shapes.

Most letters are slightly wider at the top

Consistent spaces between double strokes

Oval-curl foot

LETTER-SPACING GUIDE

All letters sit on the baseline. See page 12 for more information on letter spacing.

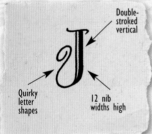

Double-stroked vertical

Quirky letter shapes

12 nib widths high

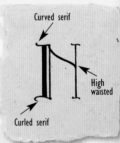

Curved serif

Curled serif

High waisted

LETTER CONSTRUCTION: J

1 Beginning at the top, draw a vertical stroke using a fine-line marker.

2 Use a calligraphy marker at a 0° angle to add a parallel stroke. Curve and taper to the left about three-quarters of the way down.

3 Using the fine-line marker, draw an oval curl. End the stroke so that it overlaps the end of the previous stroke.

4 Use the fine-line marker to add a serif.

LETTER CONSTRUCTION: N

1 Beginning at the top, use a calligraphy marker at a 0° angle to make a vertical line.

2 Add a parallel stroke with a fine-line marker. Determine the width of the letter and add a second parallel line.

3 Use the fine-line marker to add a slightly curved line, joining the two fine downstrokes above center height.

4 Use the fine-line marker to add curved serifs.

0° dominant pen angle

12 nib widths

capital height

baseline

GRANDMA'S HANDWRITING

Nothing looks more sincere than a handwritten note. This alphabet reminds us of a time when personal handwriting was the only way to send a love letter or thank you note. Follow the exemplar shown on the opposite page or practice your own handwriting; use the same tool to create lettering in different sizes. Use Grandma's Handwriting for labels or longer heartfelt expressions of love and admiration for those you cherish.

NOTE TO SCRAPBOOKERS Use Grandma's Handwriting Capitals (pages 34–35) as the uppercase letters for this alphabet.

TOOLS
0.50 mm pigmented fine-line marker

Alternative tools:
Pencil, ballpoint pen, colored pencil, or colored marker

DISTINGUISHING FEATURES

The letter shapes are generally oval, and although it is a running hand, some letters are not joined. A number of letters include a small curl, and most of the ascenders and descenders are looped. Fairly consistent letter slant and repeated letter shapes make the writing more attractive. There are a number of inconsistencies within this alphabet—a testimony to the unique nature of each person's own handwriting.

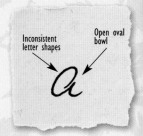

Inconsistent letter shapes

Open oval bowl

LETTER-SPACING GUIDE

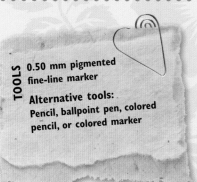

Some letters are not joined. See page 12 for more information on letter spacing.

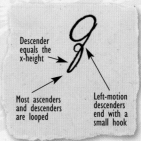

Descender equals the x-height

Most ascenders and descenders are looped

Left-motion descenders end with a small hook

Some ascenders and descenders have no loop

Most ascenders equal the x-height

30° letter slant

LETTER CONSTRUCTION: R

1 Begin with a slanted upward stroke, making it slightly curved.

2 Continue around to create a fairly significant top loop.

3 Continue the stroke, making a shoulder and then dropping down toward the baseline on a 30° slant.

4 Exit by pulling right, keeping almost parallel to the baseline.

LETTER CONSTRUCTION: W

1 Begin with a slightly curved upward stroke at a slant of about 30°.

2 Retrace briefly before making the first valley, ending at about three-quarters of the x-height.

3 Continue by retracing briefly and then forming the second valley, ending just above the x-height.

4 Finish by pulling to the right and slightly upward.

30° letter
slant

a b c d e f

g h i j k l

m n o p q r

s t u v w x

y z ! ? 1 2 3

4 5 6 7 8 9 0

ascender ↑
x-height
baseline
descender ↓

* Where there are no numbers, the letter is drawn with one continuous stroke.

GRANDMA'S HANDWRITING CAPITALS

These letters should only be used as capital letters with the lowercase Grandma's Handwriting. Large uppercase letters make handwriting more legible and provide welcome resting places in a long body of text. This alphabet features some traditional letter forms, but you can substitute your own if you wish; try to be consistent within a single project. You can use the same tool to write this alphabet in different sizes.

NOTE TO SCRAPBOOKERS Use Grandma's Handwriting (pages 32–33) as the lowercase letters and numbers for this alphabet.

TOOLS

0.50 mm pigmented fine-line marker

Alternative tools: Pencil, ballpoint pen, colored pencil, or colored marker

DISTINGUISHING FEATURES

This alphabet is written at a letter slant of approximately 30°. You may be more comfortable with a different slant; what is important is to be fairly consistent. These traditional letters have large oval flourishes, and some have the same small curl at the base of the vertical that is found on the accompanying lowercase alphabet. A number of these letters graduate down toward the right, emphasizing the letter slant.

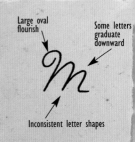

Large oval flourish

Some letters graduate downward

Inconsistent letter shapes

LETTER-SPACING GUIDE

This uppercase alphabet was designed for use only with the lowercase letters, not to be used alone. These three spacing examples demonstrate some upper- and lowercase letters together.

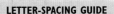

See page 12 for more information on letter spacing.

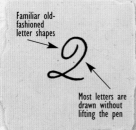

Familiar old-fashioned letter shapes

Most letters are drawn without lifting the pen

30° letter slant

Some letters have descenders

LETTER CONSTRUCTION: W

1 Begin by drawing a large oval curl and then a diagonal line at about 30° extending down to the baseline.

2 Continue with an upward diagonal that ends at about three-quarters of the letter height.

3 Draw another diagonal parallel to the first one.

4 Complete the letter with a curved diagonal extending up to about half the letter height.

LETTER CONSTRUCTION: K

1 Begin by drawing a large oval curl, then continue down at an angle of about 30°. At the baseline, bounce up and draw a short curl.

2 Start the second stroke with a slight curve, then loop it around the first stroke at about half the letter height.

3 Continue the second stroke diagonally down to the baseline, ending with a small curl. Note the slight curves.

30° letter
slant

A B C D E
F G H I J K
L M N O P
Q R S T U
V W X Y & Z

capital height
baseline

MADELINE

This is a lighthearted and versatile alphabet with a casual feel. It is easy to learn and fun to write, and can be drawn with any monoline tool. This letter style can be used to record everyday fun, birthday parties, or pet adventures. Text can be adapted to your page by tucking in a smaller letter here and there, or by extending a kick-leg at the end of a line. To adjust the size of this alphabet, simply use finer- or heavier-weight writing tools.

NOTE TO SCRAPBOOKERS Use Madeline Capitals (pages 38–39) as the uppercase letters for this alphabet.

TOOLS
0.70 mm pigmented fine-line marker

Alternative tools: Experiment to see what weights and colors are most appropriate for your project; try pencils, markers, or gel pens.

DISTINGUISHING FEATURES

This cheerful alphabet has low-branching letters, angular bowls, and a round o. Vertical strokes begin and end with casually drawn serifs. An alternate o size (shown in the letter-spacing guide below) and inconsistent serif angles allow you to improvise as you write, so that the letters can be packed quite closely together. Pulling the right leg of the a, h, m, n, and k at the end of sentences or text lines gives the alphabet a casual feel.

Low branching

Angular bowl

Descender is slightly shorter than x-height

LETTER-SPACING GUIDE

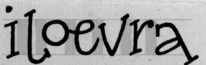

Letters dance up and down on the baseline, and some reach beyond the guidelines. The size of the o is varied to ease spacing and add visual interest. See page 12 for more information on letter spacing.

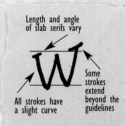

Length and angle of slab serifs vary

All strokes have a slight curve

Some strokes extend beyond the guidelines

Turn is rounded

Leg kicks out

Ascender is slightly shorter than x-height

LETTER CONSTRUCTION: K

1 Beginning at the top, draw a vertical stroke.

2 Branch out the second stroke from within the first and curl around at the tip to create a ball.

3 Start the third stroke so that it overlaps the second without touching the first. Extend the stroke slightly beyond the baseline.

4 Add serifs of varying lengths and angles.

LETTER CONSTRUCTION: Z

1 Draw the first stroke on a slight upward slope.

2 Start the second stroke so that it overlaps the first and runs diagonally down to the baseline.

3 Start the third stroke so that it overlaps the second and slopes very slightly downward.

4 Add serifs of varying lengths and angles.

ascender

x-height

baseline

descender

MADELINE CAPITALS

This alphabet is primarily intended for use with the lowercase Madeline, but can also be employed alone for casual titles and short, cheerful captions about things such as cooking with Grandma or visiting with friends. The varied heights and widths of these letters give the impression that they are skipping across the page. Use a marker with a larger tip to create larger lettering or a smaller tip for a scaled-down version of this alphabet.

NOTE TO SCRAPBOOKERS Use Madeline (pages 36–37) as the lowercase letters and numbers for this alphabet.

TOOLS 0.70 mm pigmented fine-line marker

Alternative tools: Experiment to see what weights and colors are most appropriate for your project; try pencils, markers, or gel pens.

DISTINGUISHING FEATURES

This modern monoline letter style has rounded bowls that may vary in size and verticals that are not quite straight. The carefree serifs vary in length and are often drawn at different angles. Kick-legs can be extended to fill space at the end of a line or pulled below the baseline for tighter spacing. Letters are allowed to slant slightly forward and backward to help give the alphabet a feeling of movement.

Serif is an extension of the bowl

Rounded bowls may vary in size

LETTER-SPACING GUIDE

LOCVIR

Some letters reach beyond the guidelines. See page 12 for more information on letter spacing.

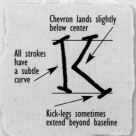

Chevron lands slightly below center

All strokes have a subtle curve

Kick-legs sometimes extend beyond baseline

Slab serifs vary in length and angle

Baseline serif may be longer to provide stability

Letters may lean slightly forward or back

LETTER CONSTRUCTION: B

1 Draw a vertical stroke from top to bottom.

2 Start the second stroke so that it overlaps the first. This bowl is slightly less than half the letter height.

3 Complete the third stroke so that it overlaps the previous two strokes.

LETTER CONSTRUCTION: N

1 Draw a vertical stroke, beginning at the top. Note that all strokes have a subtle curve to them.

2 Start the second stroke so that it overlaps the first and is slightly curved.

3 Draw the third stroke so that it ends by overlapping the second stroke.

4 Add slab serifs of varying lengths and angles.

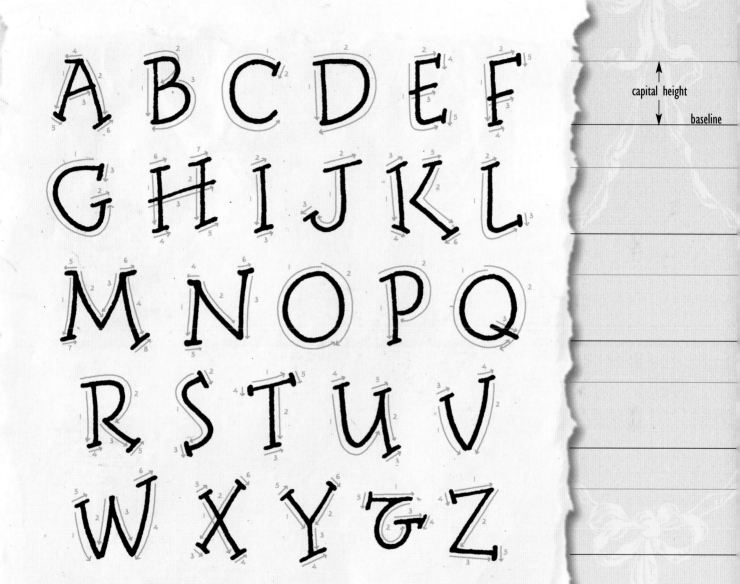

capital height

baseline

ONCE UPON A TIME

A single large capital acts as a decorative accent at the beginning of a body of text and invites the reader into the story. These letters were inspired by the traditional versals used in old manuscripts. Fill the letter shapes with any color or pattern that suits the subject you are writing about. One decorated capital is enough to set the tone for each page of your magical memories. These letters can be written in different sizes using the same tools.

NOTE TO SCRAPBOOKERS Use Roman Minuscules (pages 110–111) or Uncial (pages 114–115) as the lowercase letters and numbers for this alphabet.

DISTINGUISHING FEATURES

These large Uncial-style versals filled with color and pattern produce decorative capitals for use as a visual entry point for a body of text. The large, round, outlined letters have long serifs with swollen ends. A variety of patterns and colors are demonstrated here, but letters can be filled with any color or pattern you choose. A border of dots or scallops can be added to provide additional embellishment to the letters if desired.

TOOLS
H pencil
Colored fine-line markers
Soft white eraser

Alternative tools:
Colored pencils or gel pens

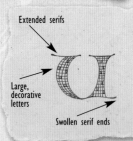

Extended serifs

Large, decorative letters

Swollen serif ends

LETTER-SPACING GUIDE

These capitals were designed for use as a single letter to accent the beginning of a body of text. Three spacing examples are shown here.

See page 12 for more information on letter spacing.

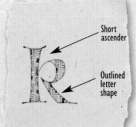

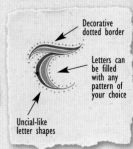

Short ascender

Outlined letter shape

Decorative dotted border

Letters can be filled with any pattern of your choice

Uncial-like letter shapes

LETTER CONSTRUCTION: B

1 Use an H pencil to sketch the letter outline.

2 Ink the outline with a fine-line marker, rotating the page whenever it is helpful. Add a little weight to the ends of the serifs.

3 Fill the letter with a pattern of your choice. Here, start with the vertical lines. Note how they are influenced by the letter shape.

4 Add the horizontal lines. Erase any noticeable pencil lines when the ink is dry, then add color to random tiles.

VARIATIONS

Alternative, more traditional capital letter forms for A, H, and T filled with new pattern ideas.

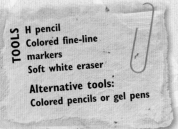

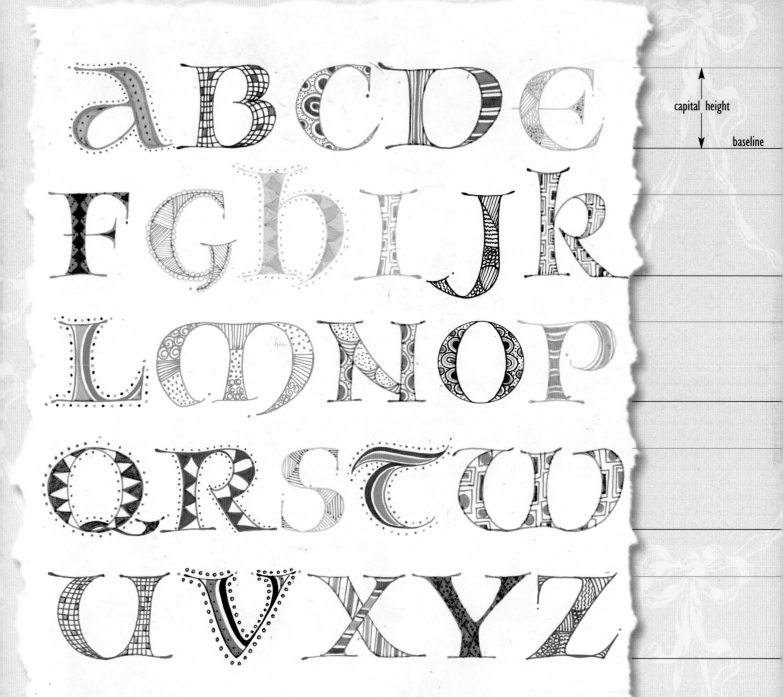

capital height

baseline

PAJAMA STRIPES

These letters are simple to draw and easy to adapt to almost any size using the same tools. Overlap the letter outlines to make words and then fill them in with your favorite flannel pattern. The alphabet can be used for captions, titles, and short phrases about lazy weekends, slumber parties, or naptime snuggles. Change the colors and patterns to fashion the letters after little sister's, big brother's, or even Daddy's PJs.

NOTE TO SCRAPBOOKERS Pajama Stripes does not require a coordinating lowercase alphabet.

TOOLS 0.42 mm pigmented fine-line marker
Colored pencils

Alternative tools:
Gel pens or colored fine-line markers

DISTINGUISHING FEATURES

These simple bubble letters can easily be modified to suit your needs. The round letter shapes are fairly consistent in height and weight, with curved corners and small counter spaces. When drawing words and phrases, allow the letters to overlap and lean on each other, then fill them with patterns and colors that remind you of pajamas.

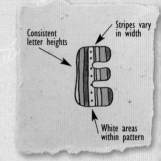

Consistent letter heights

Stripes vary in width

White areas within pattern

LETTER-SPACING GUIDE

Letters can overlap and bump into each other. Allow just enough space to make them legible.

See page 12 for more information on letter spacing.

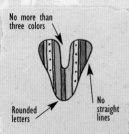

No more than three colors

Rounded letters

No straight lines

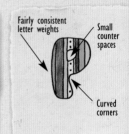

Fairly consistent letter weights

Small counter spaces

Curved corners

LETTER CONSTRUCTION: A

1 Ouline the letter with a fine-line marker. Rotate your page whenever it is helpful.

2 Add stripes of varying widths. Fill some stripes with dots or other embellishments.

3 Use colored pencils to fill in the stripes, leaving some white and using a maximum of three colors.

VARIATIONS

Pink pajamas with hearts for Sis.

Plaid pajamas for Dad.

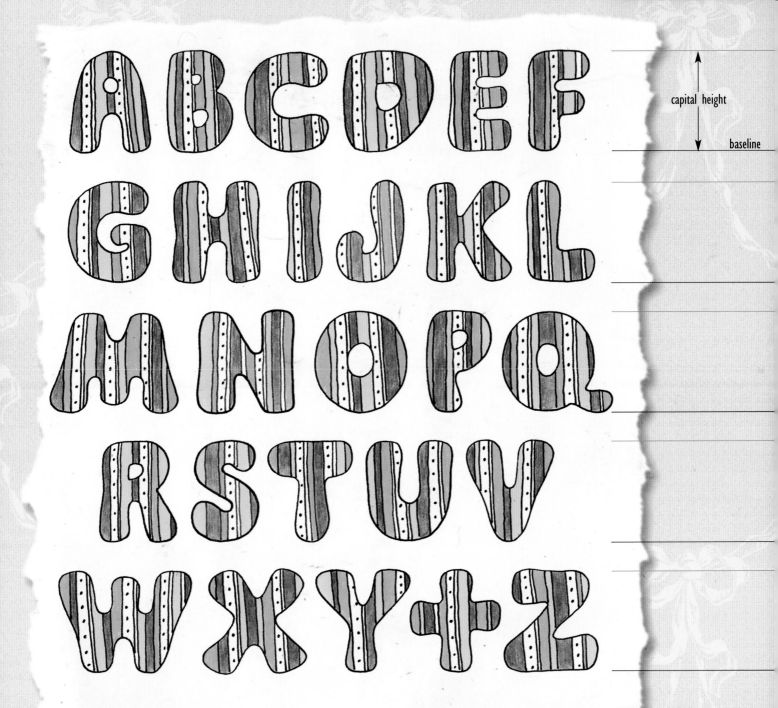

capital height

baseline

CHILD'S PLAY

Use your nonwriting hand to create a playground of happy memories. These colorful, uninhibited letters tumble across the page. There are no worries here about consistency in size, shape, or line quality. Use bright colors, mix and match upper- and lowercase letters, and include the occasional backward letter. This alphabet is fitting for stories told from a child's perspective, or for recording the surprising things that young children say.

NOTE TO SCRAPBOOKERS This is a monocase alphabet. Mix and match upper- and lowercase letters for a spontaneous look.

TOOLS
Crayons
Alternative tools:
Medium-point colored markers

DISTINGUISHING FEATURES

This is a colorful alphabet with very few rules. The only concern is to ensure that the text is readable. A mixture of upper- and lowercase letters gives the alphabet warmth, and the occasional backward letter adds an innocent charm. The letters should not be contained between guidelines. Use the baseline just as a reference for multiple lines of writing, or work without any guidelines at all, allowing words to spill across the pages in an unselfconscious way. Crooked lines and inconsistent letters are encouraged!

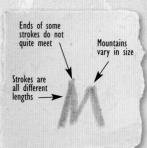

Ends of some strokes do not quite meet

Mountains vary in size

Strokes are all different lengths

LETTER-SPACING GUIDE

Letter spacing is inconsistent. Spaces between words should be greater than spacing between letters. Letters bounce along the baseline.

See page 12 for more information on letter spacing.

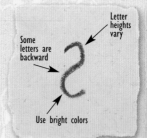

Letter heights vary

Some letters are backward

Use bright colors

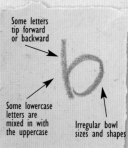

Some letters tip forward or backward

Some lowercase letters are mixed in with the uppercase

Irregular bowl sizes and shapes

LETTER CONSTRUCTION: A

1 Draw the first stroke. Try using your nonwriting hand; your letters may be quite different from those shown here.

2 Draw the second stroke, allowing it to overshoot the first where they meet.

3 Draw the final stroke so that it does not touch the first stroke but overshoots the second.

LETTER CONSTRUCTION: R

1 Draw the first vertical stroke, allowing it to tilt back a little.

2 Draw the second stroke backward.

3 Complete the kick-leg, allowing it to extend beyond the baseline.

4 It is fine to go back and add "forgotten" strokes, such as completing the bowl of the R.

A b ɔ D E f G

H I J K L M N

O p Q ʁ 2 t u

v w X Y ƨ ꙅ !

1 2 3 4 5 6 7 8 9 0

baseline

MORSE CODE

Dots and dashes suggest a text full of intrigue and coded messages. This style can be adapted to incorporate an endless variety of motifs to suit your memory pages. Created with familiar tools, these letters are easy but time consuming to draw. Carefully sketch words lightly in pencil to provide a guide before adding the dots and dashes. This alphabet can easily be adapted for larger titles by using slightly larger pens.

NOTE TO SCRAPBOOKERS Use Schoolbook Capitals (pages 118–119) in conjunction with the instructions given here to create an uppercase Morse Code alphabet.

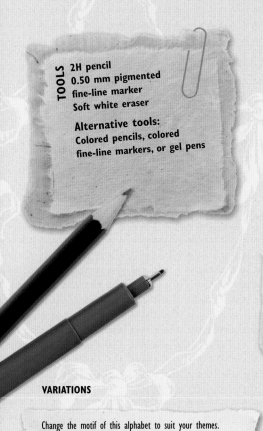

TOOLS
2H pencil
0.50 mm pigmented fine-line marker
Soft white eraser

Alternative tools:
Colored pencils, colored fine-line markers, or gel pens

DISTINGUISHING FEATURES

Morse Code is based on the Schoolbook alphabet to ensure legibility, so refer to pages 116–117 for guidance on drawing the underlying letter shapes. The dots and dashes are added quickly but carefully, giving the alphabet an interesting texture. Vertical letters with round bowls have ascenders and descenders that are equal in length to the letter's x-height. This alphabet can be adapted for an endless variety of themes by substituting other small, simple motifs for the dots and dashes.

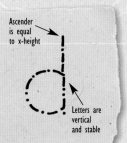

Motif carefully follows Schoolbook letter shape

Arch extends from just below the top of the vertical

Descender is equal to x-height

Round bowl breaks into the guidelines

Ascender is equal to x-height

Letters are vertical and stable

LETTER-SPACING GUIDE

All letters sit on the baseline.

See page 12 for more information on letter spacing.

VARIATIONS

Change the motif of this alphabet to suit your themes. Here are a few suggestions to help spark your imagination.

Pebbles   Cookie cutter   Patio lights   Stitches

LETTER CONSTRUCTION: K

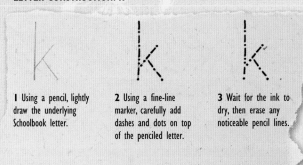

1 Using a pencil, lightly draw the underlying Schoolbook letter.

2 Using a fine-line marker, carefully add dashes and dots on top of the penciled letter.

3 Wait for the ink to dry, then erase any noticeable pencil lines.

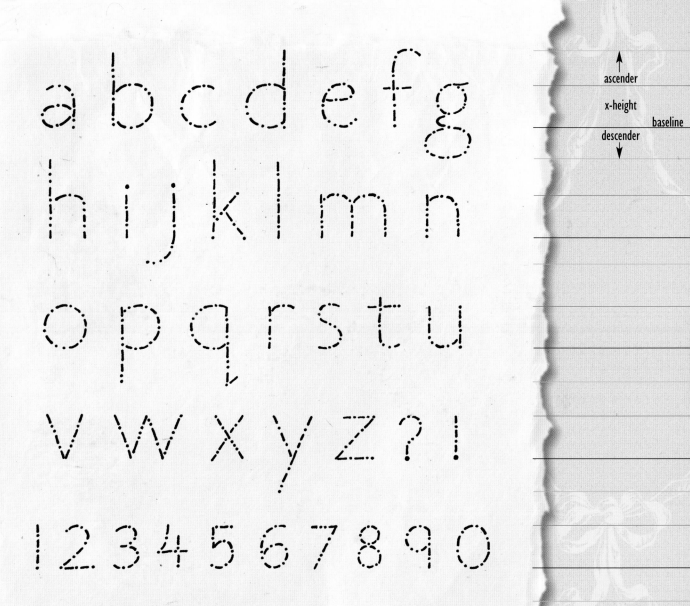

ascender
x-height
baseline
descender

APPLIQUÉ

These cheerful letters will brighten up your scrapbook pages. The letters are drawn, outlined, and filled in with a decorative element to give them a layered look. A variety of motifs are demonstrated here, but you can use any color or pattern that suits your mood, as well as vary the size using the same tools. Lettering will look more homogenous if only one motif and a limited color palette are used within a single body of text.

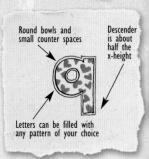

NOTE TO SCRAPBOOKERS Adapt the letter shapes of Schoolbook Capitals (pages 118–119) to use as uppercase letters for Appliqué.

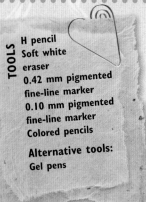

TOOLS
H pencil
Soft white eraser
0.42 mm pigmented fine-line marker
0.10 mm pigmented fine-line marker
Colored pencils

Alternative tools:
Gel pens

DISTINGUISHING FEATURES

The letters are sketched lightly with pencil before being drawn with a fine-line marker and then outlined with a finer marker. The extra-fine outline gives the letters a layered look and adds a sweet handmade touch to this alphabet. The letters are upright and fairly consistent in shape, with round bowls and small counter spaces. Ascenders and descenders are about half the length of the x-height.

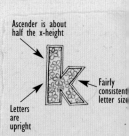

Round bowls and small counter spaces

Descender is about half the x-height

Letters can be filled with any pattern of your choice

LETTER-SPACING GUIDE

All letters sit on the baseline. See page 12 for more information on letter spacing.

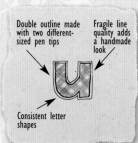

Double outline made with two different-sized pen tips

Fragile line quality adds a handmade look

Consistent letter shapes

Ascender is about half the x-height

Letters are upright

Fairly consistent letter size

LETTER CONSTRUCTION: S

1 Use an H pencil to sketch the letter outline.

2 Ink in the letter shape with a fine-line marker, rotating the page whenever it is helpful.

3 Outline the letter with a finer marker. When the ink is dry, erase any noticeable pencil lines.

4 Fill in the letter with a motif of your choice. Notice that the finished letter is larger than the original pencil outline.

VARIATIONS

Alternate letter shapes for y, a, and w. Use a similar x and v when using this w. Try using texture instead of color to fill the letters.

ascender

x-height

baseline

descender

BEACH FUN

This alphabet gets its playful feel from the way in which the organic letter shapes seem to dance and sway within the guidelines. It is appropriate for scrapbook pages about outdoor fun, barbecue parties, or beach vacations. This style is easy to learn, and fun to write. It can be written in a variety of sizes with the same markers. In order to maintain the energetic feel of this alphabet, always use two markers with significant contrast in line width.

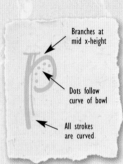

Branches at mid x-height

Dots follow curve of bowl

All strokes are curved

NOTE TO SCRAPBOOKERS Use Beach Fun Capitals (pages 52–53) as the uppercase letters for this alphabet.

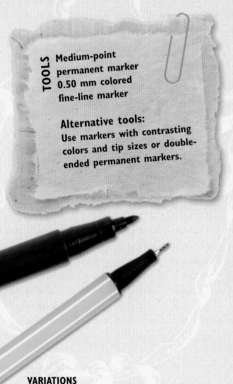

TOOLS Medium-point permanent marker 0.50 mm colored fine-line marker

Alternative tools:
Use markers with contrasting colors and tip sizes or double-ended permanent markers.

DISTINGUISHING FEATURES

A feeling of movement is achieved by varying the size of the letters and by allowing some of them to extend above and below the baseline. However, the majority of letters in each word should stay on the baseline so that the text remains grounded. The basic letter shapes are drawn with the larger-tipped marker and then they are loosely double-stroked and embellished with the fine-tipped marker. Vary the size and placement of dots and sunrays in order to avoid elements that crash into each other. A subtle curve in all the letter strokes adds to this alphabet's carefree air.

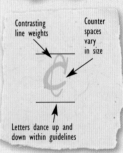

Contrasting line weights

Counter spaces vary in size

Letters dance up and down within guidelines

LETTER-SPACING GUIDE

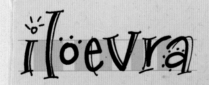

Smaller letters are raised above the baseline and occasionally a letter falls below it, but the majority sit on the baseline to give the words some stability. See page 12 for more information on letter spacing.

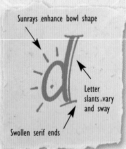

Sunrays enhance bowl shape

Letter slants vary and sway

Swollen serif ends

VARIATIONS

Change the embellishments.

Vary the letter sizes.

Use a single color.

LETTER CONSTRUCTION: X

1 Use a medium-point marker to draw the first base stroke.

2 Complete the second stroke. Notice that the lines have a slight curve to them.

3 Mirror the first stroke using a fine-line marker.

4 Use the fine-line marker to add serifs and dots.

ascender

x-height

baseline

descender

Alternate letter forms

BEACH FUN CAPITALS

These letters have the feel of sun, sand, and surf and are just the ticket for recording memories of a sunshine getaway. Use them alone for titles and accent words, or with the lowercase Beach Fun letters. This style combines the line widths of two different markers, and can be written at a variety of sizes without changing tools. Play with the letter slant and embellishments in this alphabet, but limit yourself to two or three colors per layout.

NOTE TO SCRAPBOOKERS Use Beach Fun (pages 50–51) as the lowercase letters and numbers for this alphabet.

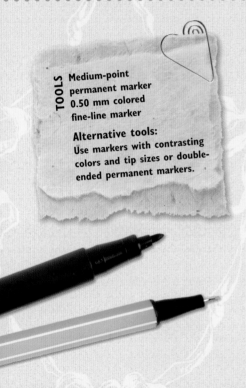

TOOLS Medium-point permanent marker 0.50 mm colored fine-line marker

Alternative tools: Use markers with contrasting colors and tip sizes or double-ended permanent markers.

DISTINGUISHING FEATURES

The letters are made more dynamic by drawing them with two different-sized pen tips. The basic strokes are made with the heavier-tipped marker and then loosely double-stroked and embellished with the finer-tipped pen. A feeling of movement is created by allowing the letters to tilt forward and backward and by extending some strokes slightly beyond the guidelines. Vary the size and placement of dots or sunrays so that the embellishments do not crash into each other. There are practically no straight lines in this alphabet—even the straight strokes have a bit of a curve to them.

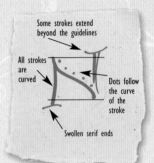

Some strokes extend beyond the guidelines

All strokes are curved

Dots follow the curve of the stroke

Swollen serif ends

LETTER-SPACING GUIDE

Some letters reach beyond the guidelines.

See page 12 for more information on letter spacing.

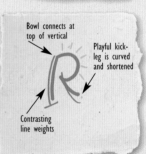

Bowl connects at top of vertical

Playful kick-leg is curved and shortened

Contrasting line weights

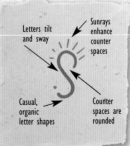

Letters tilt and sway

Sunrays enhance counter spaces

Casual, organic letter shapes

Counter spaces are rounded

VARIATIONS

Vary the embellishments.

Allow the letters to tilt and sway.

Vary the colors.

LETTER CONSTRUCTION: K

1 Beginning at the top, draw the first base stroke using a medium-point marker.

2 Add the second stroke. Notice that the lines have a slight curve to them and the leg stroke kicks out.

3 Use a fine-line marker to double-stroke the letter.

4 Add serifs and dots with the fine-line marker.

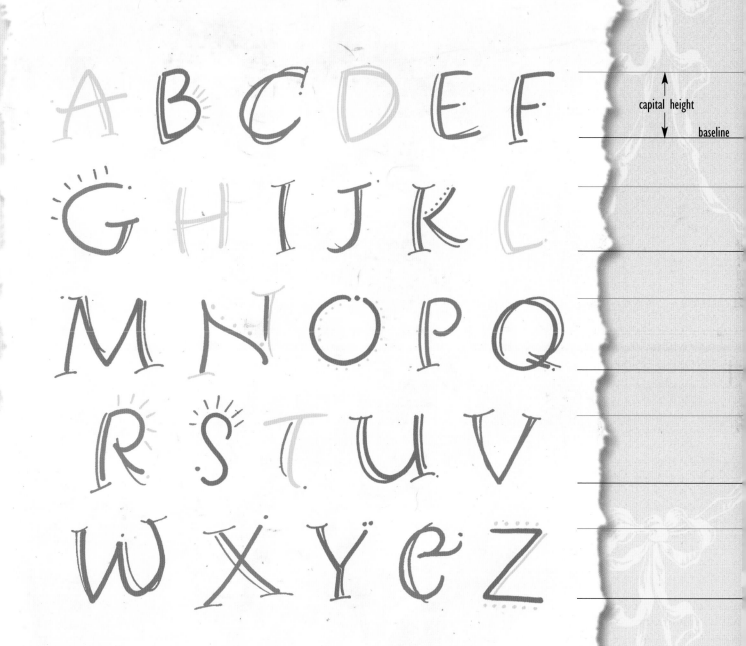

capital height

baseline

FLOWER POWER

Little flowers are used in this alphabet to create a delightful garden of words. This style is perfect for recording the sweet memories of innocence and first loves. Easy but time consuming, the letters are drawn with familiar tools. Carefully sketch words lightly in pencil to provide a guide before adding the flowers. The same tools can be used to draw this alphabet in larger sizes.

NOTE TO SCRAPBOOKERS Use Schoolbook Capitals (pages 118–119) in conjunction with the instructions given here to create an uppercase Flower Power alphabet.

TOOLS

2H pencil
Gel pen
0.30 mm colored fine-line marker
Soft white eraser

Alternative tools:
Colored pencils will create a softer look. Sharpen the pencils frequently to produce finer lines.

DISTINGUISHING FEATURES

Flower Power is based on the Schoolbook alphabet to ensure legibility, so refer to pages 116–117 for guidance on drawing the underlying letter shapes. Tiny flowers are drawn quickly but carefully, giving the alphabet a sweet feeling of innocence. Vertical letters with round bowls have ascenders and descenders that are equal in length to the x-height. A larger flower is used on the a, g, and 8, where counter spaces might become too congested by a ring of smaller flowers.

LETTER-SPACING GUIDE

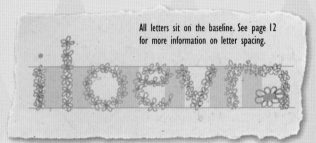

All letters sit on the baseline. See page 12 for more information on letter spacing.

Use a single large flower to create smaller bowls

Dots are placed accurately along the penciled letter

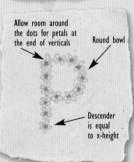

Allow room around the dots for petals at the end of verticals

Round bowl

Descender is equal to x-height

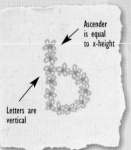

Ascender is equal to x-height

Letters are vertical

VARIATIONS

Vary the sizes of the flowers.

Use two colors for the flowers.

LETTER CONSTRUCTION: A

1 Using a pencil, lightly draw the underlying Schoolbook letter.

2 Use a gel pen to draw a large spot in the center of the bowl, then space smaller dots evenly along the penciled letter.

3 Using a fine-line marker in a contrasting color, draw large flower petals to create the bowl shape.

4 Use the marker to draw small petals around each dot. Wait for the ink to dry, then erase any noticeable pencil lines.

ascender

x-height

baseline

descender

ART DECO

Traditional round letters can be given an Art Deco appearance when a substantial contrast in line weights is used. This alphabet has the feel of high society during the Roaring Twenties. Use this letter style for labels and text about old black-and-white photos of Grandma, classic automobiles, or special outings to the theater to give your pages the jazzy, upscale feel of Broadway. To adjust the size of the alphabet, use finer- or heavier-weight markers.

NOTE TO SCRAPBOOKERS Use Art Deco Capitals (pages 58–59) as the uppercase letters for this alphabet.

TOOLS
5.0 mm pigmented calligraphy marker
0.50 mm pigmented fine-line marker

Alternative tools:
Traditional broad-edged dip pen and calligraphy fountain pen

DISTINGUISHING FEATURES

The bold vertical strokes are made with a calligraphy marker at an x-height of just over 2 nib widths and are complemented by horizontal lines and round bowls that are carefully drawn with a fine-line marker. These letters sit comfortably on the baseline and have round bowls of consistent size that break into the guidelines. Portions of a, c, e, g, and o require shading equal in width to the calligraphic tip. The top-left corners of some diagonal strokes also need to be drawn and filled in. Ascenders and descenders are equal to the x-height.

Corner is drawn and filled in

Alternate strokes are parallel

LETTER-SPACING GUIDE

All letters sit on the baseline. See page 12 for more information on letter spacing.

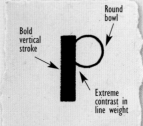

Round bowl

Bold vertical stroke

Extreme contrast in line weight

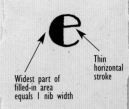

Widest part of filled-in area equals 1 nib width

Thin horizontal stroke

LETTER CONSTRUCTION: V

I Using a calligraphy marker at a 65° angle, pull the first stroke downward.

2 Use a fine-line marker to draw a line that extends along the edge of the first stroke and up to the guideline.

3 Use the fine-line marker to draw the upper corner of the first stroke.

4 Fill in the corner with the marker.

LETTER CONSTRUCTION: A

I Using a fine-line marker, make the top of the first stroke almost flat.

2 Draw an oval bowl about three-quarters of the x-height. Let it overlap and extend slightly beyond the first stroke.

3 Use a calligraphy marker to measure the width of the shaded area, allowing the nib to overlap the bowl outline.

4 Use the fine-line marker to fill in the shaded area.

0° dominant pen angle (all other angles are indicated next to the stroke)

2+ nib widths

2+ nib widths

2+ nib widths

ascender

x-height

baseline

descender

Indicates area that requires shading (see letter construction guidelines)

ART DECO CAPITALS

This Art Deco-inspired alphabet can be used alone for titles and short captions, or with the lowercase Art Deco for longer pieces of text. These stylized letters have big impact and need to be written slowly and carefully to ensure a slick, uptown look. Use finer- or heavier-weight tools to create the letters in different sizes. Some letters require shading, and the corners of the diagonal letters need to be drawn and filled in.

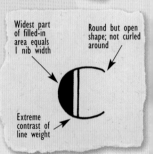

NOTE TO SCRAPBOOKERS Use Art Deco (pages 56–57) as the lowercase letters and numbers for this alphabet.

TOOLS

5.0 mm pigmented calligraphy marker
0.50 mm pigmented fine-line marker

Alternative tools:
Traditional broad-edged dip pen and calligraphy fountain pen

Distinguishing features

These very consistent block letters line up carefully along the baseline. Wide vertical strokes are accented with contrasting fine lines and large, round bowls. Notice the elegant high-waisting and the gentle upward curve in the K and the bowls of B, P, and R. Also note the short lines that connect the fine strokes to the wide ones. The heavy verticals are drawn 4 nib-widths high with a flat pen angle. Allow the gentle curve of round letters and the valley points of the W to break the baseline.

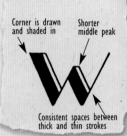

Widest part of filled-in area equals I nib width

Round but open shape; not curled around

Extreme contrast of line weight

LETTER-SPACING GUIDE

All letters sit on the baseline. Each letter acts as a block or unit. The units are placed side by side, with the exception of I, which should be given the same unit space as L.

See page 12 for more information on letter spacing.

Heavy stroke equals I nib width

Curled stroke adds charm

High waisted

Corner is drawn and shaded in

Shorter middle peak

Consistent spaces between thick and thin strokes

LETTER CONSTRUCTION: V

I Using a calligraphy marker at a 50° pen angle, pull the first downward stroke.

2 Use a fine-line marker to extend the second stroke upward from the angle at the bottom of the first stroke.

3 Use the fine-line marker to add a thin line parallel to the heavy stroke, then draw the corner and connecting stroke.

4 Fill in the corner shading with the fine-line marker.

LETTER CONSTRUCTION: S

I Using a calligraphy marker, make the first stroke, maintaining a flat pen angle throughout.

2 Use a fine-line marker to add a thin parallel stroke that joins the first stroke smoothly at the top and bottom.

3 Use the fine-line marker to add a top thin stroke. Do not extend it as wide as the bottom bowl.

4 Add the bottom thin stroke, extending it only as wide as the top bowl.

0° dominant pen angle (all other angles are indicated next to the stroke)

4 nib widths

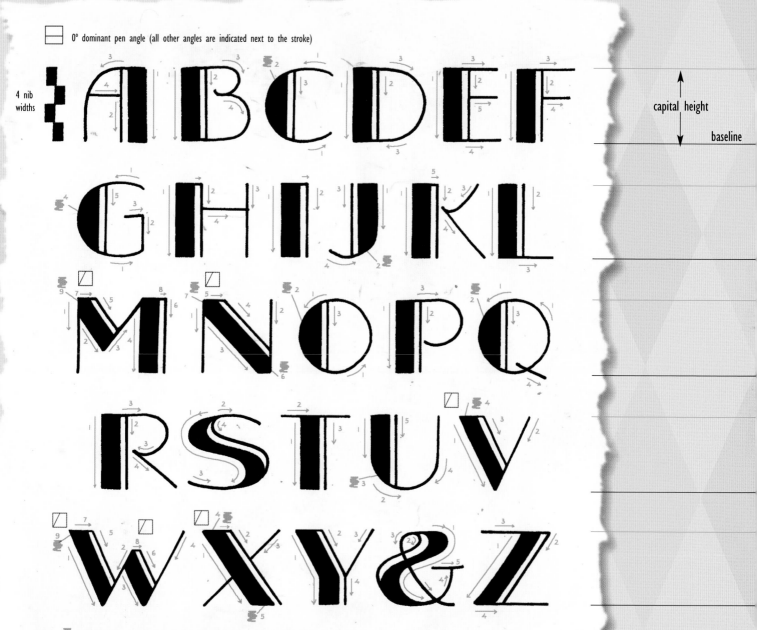

capital height

baseline

Indicates area that requires shading (see letter construction guidelines)

HAIRY

This lighthearted alphabet can be used for titles or captions about first haircuts, crazy costumes, pet stories, or bad-hair days. Use the letters as decorative capitals with Schoolbook (pages 116–117) for longer sentences. With a little imagination, the hairstyles can be altered to suit your stories. This alphabet can easily be adapted for larger titles by using slightly larger-tipped pens.

NOTE TO SCRAPBOOKERS Use Schoolbook (pages 116–117) in conjunction with the instructions given here to create a lowercase Hairy alphabet and numbers.

TOOLS
2H pencil
0.50 mm pigmented fine-line marker
Soft white eraser

Alternative tools:
Colored fine-line markers

DISTINGUISHING FEATURES

Hairy is based on the Schoolbook Capitals alphabet to ensure legibility, so refer to pages 118–119 for guidance on drawing the underlying letter shapes. Hair is added to the letter shapes quickly but carefully, to make comical letters that help illustrate your stories. All the letters can be adapted to hairstyles of your choice. This example demonstrates a variety of styles to help curl your imagination.

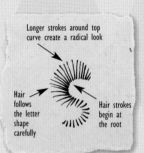

Longer strokes around top curve create a radical look

Hair follows the letter shape carefully

Hair strokes begin at the root

LETTER-SPACING GUIDE

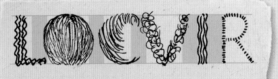

All letters sit on the baseline. See page 12 for more information on letter spacing.

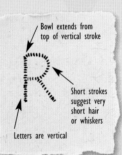

Bowl extends from top of vertical stroke

Short strokes suggest very short hair or whiskers

Letters are vertical

Occasional unruly hairs

Round, open counter space aids legibility

LETTER CONSTRUCTION: C

1 Using a 2H pencil., lightly draw the underlying Schoolbook Capitals letter.

2 Use a fine-line marker to add longer hairs. Begin each stroke on the pencil line so that the letter shape is well-defined.

3 Add shorter hairs with the fine-line marker, beginning all strokes at the "root" of the hair.

4 Wait for the ink to dry, then erase any noticeable pencil lines.

LETTER CONSTRUCTION: P

1 Using a 2H pencil., lightly draw the underlying Schoolbook Capitals letter.

2 Use a fine-line marker to add short, curved strokes to the vertical. Stagger the strokes slightly, keeping the pencil line centered in the braid.

3 Curve the braid around the bowl, again keeping it centered on the pencil line. Turn the paper if needed. Draw the end of the pigtail.

4 Wait for the ink to dry, then erase any noticeable pencil lines.

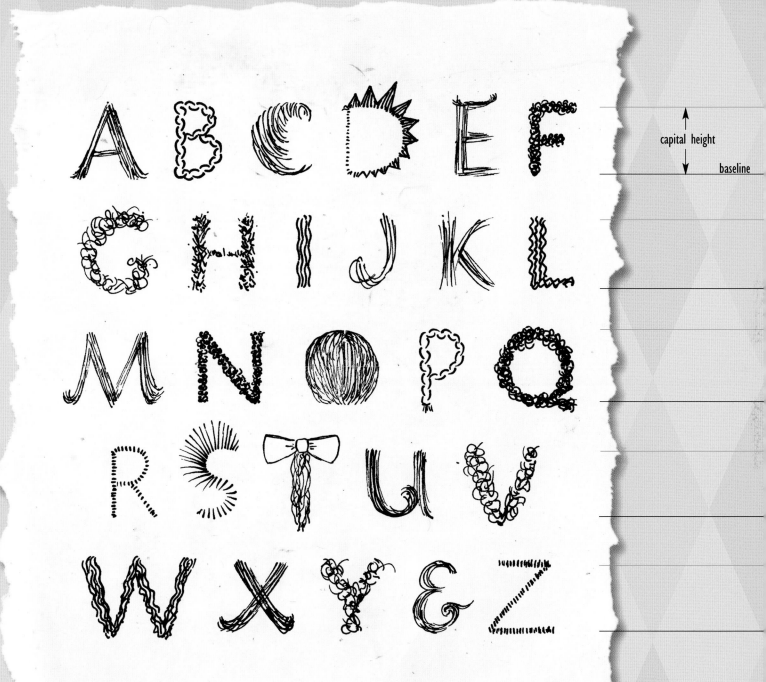

capital height

baseline

CURLS

Curls in all the right places give these carefully drawn, dancing letters a touch of whimsy. Use this letter style any time you have an upbeat but informal event to remember, such as an afternoon tea party or a bridal shower invitation or scrapbook page. This alphabet can be written in a variety of sizes using the same tools. Mix and match pencil colors to accent the décor in your pictures.

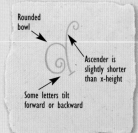

NOTE TO SCRAPBOOKERS Use Curls Capitals (pages 64–65) as the uppercase letters for this alphabet.

TOOLS Colored pencils

Alternative tools: Fine-line markers or gel pens

DISTINGUISHING FEATURES

Curls is a monoline alphabet with no straight lines. Tilting the letters forward and backward while they remain on the baseline creates a feeling of movement. Mid x-height branching letters have oval bowls that are fairly consistent in size and shape, and often burst through the guidelines. Larger curls are included where they will not interfere with letter spacing, and smaller curls are added to the letter stems. Ascenders and descenders are slightly shorter than the x-height, and most verticals have a single bottom serif for stability.

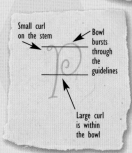

Small curl on the stem

Bowl bursts through the guidelines

Large curl is within the bowl

LETTER-SPACING GUIDE

See page 12 for more information on letter spacing.

Letters lean forward and back. Some letters extend beyond the guidelines.

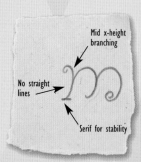

Mid x-height branching

No straight lines

Serif for stability

LETTER CONSTRUCTION: A

I Begin the first stroke just below the top guideline and curl around.

2 Start the second stroke so that it overlaps the first. The bowl is just over half the x-height and extends left, beyond the first stroke.

3 Add a short serif to the bottom of the first stroke. Note that the serif is not parallel to the baseline.

LETTER CONSTRUCTION: M

I Begin the first stroke just below the top guideline and curl around.

2 Start the second stroke so that it overlaps the first, and curl the end of the stroke slightly above the baseline.

3 Start the third stroke so that it overlaps the second and ends in a tight curl.

4 Add a short serif to the bottom of the first stroke.

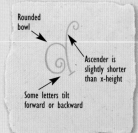

Rounded bowl

Ascender is slightly shorter than x-height

Some letters tilt forward or backward

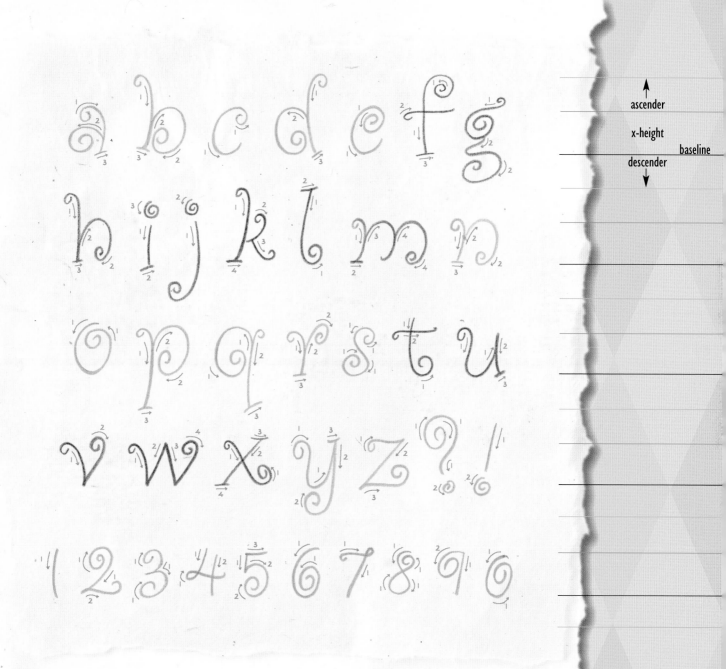

ascender

x-height

baseline

descender

CURLS CAPITALS

Designed for use with the lowercase Curls letters, these capitals add a touch of class to this whimsical alphabet. It is perfect for creating invitations or recording social events such as garden parties, baby showers, or a teddy bear picnic. These letters can easily be adapted to a variety of sizes without even changing your writing tool. All you have to do is alter the pencil color to suit the event or to match your invitation or scrapbook's color scheme.

NOTE TO SCRAPBOOKERS
Use Curls (pages 62–63) as the lowercase letters and numbers for this alphabet.

TOOLS
Colored pencils

Alternative tools:
Fine-line markers or gel pens

DISTINGUISHING FEATURES

Curls Capitals is written slowly and carefully using colored pencils. All letters sit on the baseline, although large oval bowls break through the guidelines slightly. Larger curls act as flourishes, while smaller curls and serifs are added to the letter stems to provide balance and stability. Notice that all the lines in this alphabet have a slight curve to them. Although this alphabet was written at a 30° slant, the slant should be varied when used with the lowercase letters.

Large curls serve as flourishes

Upper bowl is smaller than lower bowl

Curves break through the guidelines

LETTER-SPACING GUIDE

This uppercase alphabet was designed for use only with the lowercase letters, not to be used alone. These three spacing examples demonstrate some upper- and lowercase letters together. See page 12 for more information on letter spacing.

Serif provides stability

Slightly curved lines

Smaller curl for balance

LETTER CONSTRUCTION: K

1 Begin the first stroke just below the guideline, curling it around and then curving gently downward.

2 Begin the second stroke with a large curl, loop it at about mid-height, and end with a small curl.

3 Add a serif to the bottom of the first stroke for stability.

LETTER CONSTRUCTION: F

1 Begin the first stroke just below the guideline and curl around. Notice the slight curve in the downstroke.

2 Starting the second stroke within the first, branch up and around to make a large curl.

3 Start the third crossbar stroke with a tight curl and then cross the first stroke at about mid-height.

4 Add a serif to the bottom of the first stroke for stability.

30° letter slant can be varied when combined with lowercase letters

Large oval bowl

Oval curls echo oval letter shape

capital height

baseline

GLADIATOR

These mighty letters look as though they have survived a few battles. They are drawn with graphite pencil and have a shadow to give them the look of three-dimensional stone. Gladiator can be used for titles, captions, and short phrases about victorious teams, weathered warriors, or little heroes who have conquered life's challenges. This alphabet can be drawn at any size using the same pencils, but it is more effective at larger sizes.

NOTE TO SCRAPBOOKERS Gladiator does not require a coordinating lowercase alphabet.

TOOLS
HB pencil
2B pencil

Alternative tools:
Colored pencils

DISTINGUISHING FEATURES

The letters are outlined first with an HB pencil, and then a 2B pencil is used to soften corners and edges. The letters are bold and have a shadow for a stable, three-dimensional look. Cracks and pitting are added to both the face and shadow of each letter, so that they will look like weathered stone. They are consistent in size and shape, and stand firmly on the baseline.

Consistent letter size

Shading adds 3D effect

Use of graphite pencil adds to stone look

LETTER-SPACING GUIDE

All letters sit on the baseline. Each letter acts as a block or unit. The units are placed side by side, with the exception of I, which should be given the same unit space as the L. See page 12 for more information on letter spacing.

Both face and shadow areas are "aged"

Cracks add to aged look

Consistent shadow width

Pitting adds to stone look

Stable bottom

Corners and edges are softened

LETTER CONSTRUCTION: N

1 Lightly outline the letter shape with an HB pencil.

2 Add lines to indicate depth. Rotate the page whenever it is helpful.

3 Use a 2B pencil to add shading and soften corners and edges.

4 Add cracks and pitting to the letter's face, then add shading.

VARIATIONS

Create an O from a gladiator's shield.

An adapted lower leg and foot forms an L shape.

Two swords create a strong V.

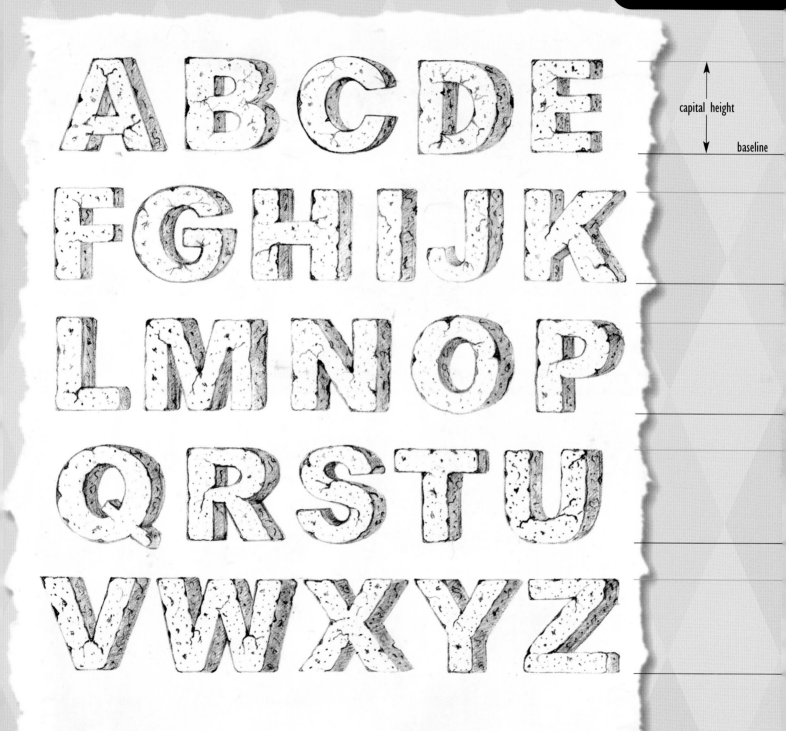

capital height

baseline

GOBLIN

These spooky faces, daggers, and ghostly shapes are designed to creep across your Halloween pages. Shaky hands and uneven strokes only add more spirit to this spine-chilling alphabet, which is created by wiggling and twisting the marker as you write. Goblin can be used for captions, short texts, and titles. Change the size of your writing tool if you would like to draw these letters in a different size.

NOTE TO SCRAPBOOKERS Use Miss Barrett (pages 86–87) in conjunction with the instructions given here to create a lowercase Goblin alphabet and numbers.

TOOLS
3.5 mm pigmented calligraphy marker

Alternative tools:
Calligraphy fountain pen

DISTINGUISHING FEATURES

These letters are constructed with jagged strokes and face-shaped bowls. Thick and thin strokes create severe contrast, and strokes that taper from wide to narrow suggest ghostly images. Wiggle the tool back and forth as you write to create shaky lines, and make scary O and Q faces quickly and easily with a few short turns of the marker. Consistency in letter height and bowl shapes will help maintain this alphabet's readability.

Shaky strokes

Strokes are tapered from top to bottom

Shape suggests a dagger

LETTER-SPACING GUIDE

All letters sit on the baseline.

See page 12 for more information on letter spacing.

Face-shaped bowl is wider at top than bottom

Ghostly features

Severe contrast in stroke weights

Tall, narrow letter shape

Jagged strokes

LETTER CONSTRUCTION: K

1 Begin at the top with a flat pen angle. Roll the marker counterclockwise between your thumb and forefinger to taper the stroke downward.

2 Wiggle the marker side to side to make a shaky second stroke. To taper the line, rotate the marker as you pull the stroke downward.

3 Start the third stroke so that it overlaps and joins the first two strokes. Notice the leg-like shape of this stroke.

LETTER CONSTRUCTION: O

1 Begin with a flat pen angle. Wiggle the marker side to side as you make the stroke.

2 Draw the second stroke so that it overlaps the first at the top but not the bottom. Note that the shape is wider at the top.

3 Add small horizontal eyes about a quarter of the way down the face.

4 Add a long tapered mouth by rotating the marker counterclockwise as you pull the stroke.

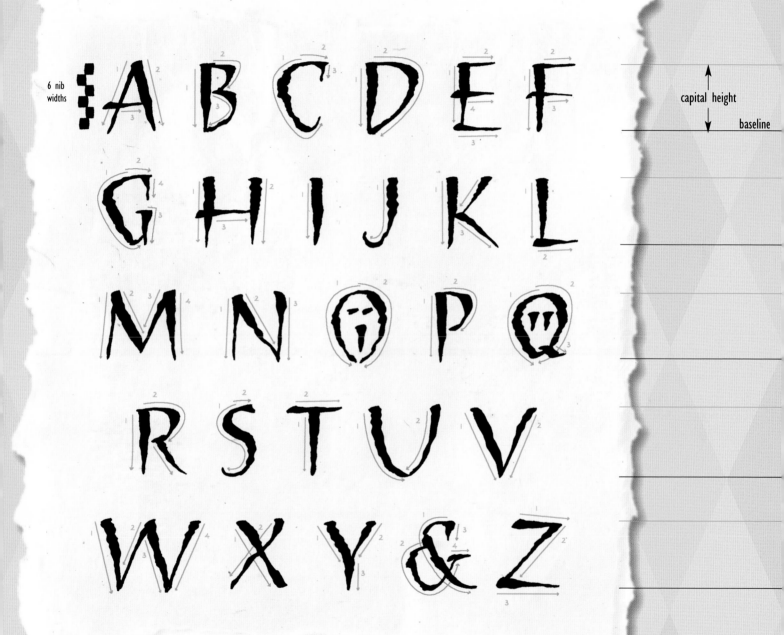

6 nib widths

capital height

baseline

STICK LETTERS

This lighthearted alphabet is fun and easy to draw. It is created using the end of a modified popsicle stick to stamp the letter strokes. Use a larger or smaller stick to create the letters in different sizes. There is no need to make perfect letters—you can line them up and space them neatly, or allow them to stumble across your page. This alphabet is great for scrapbook pages about summer camp or log cabins in the wilderness.

NOTE TO SCRAPBOOKERS Use Stick Letter Capitals (pages 72–73) as the uppercase letters for this alphabet.

TOOLS
Modified popsicle stick
Ink pad
Pigmented marker with tip equal to stick width

Tool preparation:
Cut off the round end of a popsicle stick with a pair of sharp scissors. Place some medium-grit sandpaper on a flat surface and, holding the stick vertically, sand the end to ensure that it is flat and smooth.

Distinguishing features

The letters are constructed from a series of stamped shapes. Organic-looking strokes overlap each other to create square bowls and add stability. This process often results in imperfect letters, but this just adds to the alphabet's charm. Longer strokes require an extra overlapping stamp, while some of the numbers have shorter sections that need to be drawn in with a marker. Ascenders and descenders are slightly shorter than the x-height.

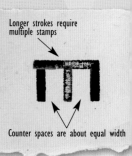

Longer strokes require multiple stamps

Counter spaces are about equal width

LETTER-SPACING GUIDE

All letters can sit on the baseline as shown, or they can tumble and skip along it. See page 12 for more information on letter spacing.

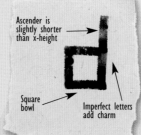

Ascender is slightly shorter than x-height

Square bowl

Imperfect letters add charm

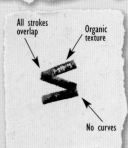

All strokes overlap

Organic texture

No curves

LETTER CONSTRUCTION: Y

1 Press the stick onto the ink pad, then stamp the first stroke on a diagonal.

2 Stamp the second stroke so that it overlaps the first. Apply more ink to the stick whenever required.

3 Apply a third stamp to extend the second stroke and form the descender.

4 Stamp a final stroke that overlaps the second stroke and extends it to the top of the x-height.

LETTER CONSTRUCTION: O

1 Press the stick onto the ink pad, then stamp the first stroke on the baseline. Apply more ink to the stick whenever required.

2 Stamp the second stroke so that it overlaps about half the width of the first stroke and aligns at the left-hand edge.

3 Apply the third stroke, overlapping and aligning it with the second stroke.

4 Complete the fourth stamp, making sure that the right-hand edges of the third and fourth strokes align.

ascender
x-height
baseline
descender

Indicates shorter sections that need to be drawn in with a marker

STICK LETTER CAPITALS

These wacky, built-up letters look like campfire kindling. Each letter is created using the sanded end of a wooden stick to stamp multiple strokes. A tongue depressor is used here, because it produces longer strokes than the popsicle stick that is used to create the coordinating lowercase alphabet. Use these laidback letters to record fireside stories, fishy tales, or memories of hiking in the great outdoors.

NOTE TO SCRAPBOOKERS Use Stick Letters (pages 70–71) as the lowercase letters and numbers for this alphabet.

TOOLS
- Modified tongue depressor
- Ink pad
- Pigmented marker with tip equal to depressor width

Tool preparation:
Cut off the round end of a tongue depressor with a pair of sharp scissors. Place some medium-grit sandpaper on a flat surface and, holding the depressor vertically, sand the end to ensure that it is flat and smooth.

DISTINGUISHING FEATURES

Stamped strokes overlap and lean on one another to create these letters. Imperfect, straight-sided shapes and triangular bowls give this alphabet its rustic look. Each stamp leaves its own organic-looking texture. Multiple stamps are required to make substantial letters, and the tongue of the Q needs to be drawn in with a marker.

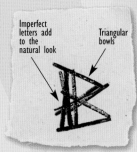

Imperfect letters add to the natural look

Triangular bowls

LETTER-SPACING GUIDE

All letters can sit on the baseline as shown, or they can tumble and skip along it. See page 12 for more information on letter spacing.

Organic texture

Multiple stamps give weight to the stroke

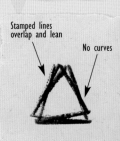

Stamped lines overlap and lean

No curves

LETTER CONSTRUCTION: P

1 Press the stick onto the ink pad, then stamp the first vertical stroke. Apply more ink to the stick whenever required.

2 Place the second stroke on an angle and allow about a quarter of its length to overhang the first stroke.

3 Complete the triangular bowl with the third stroke, allowing it to overhang the first stroke.

4 Stamp three or four more strokes to give weight to the letter. Notice that they cross and lean on each other.

LETTER CONSTRUCTION: S

1 Press the stick onto the ink pad, then stamp the first diagonal stroke within the top third of the guidelines. Apply more ink to the stick whenever required.

2 Stamp the next stroke so that it overlaps the first one and angles downward within the middle third of the guidelines.

3 Angle the third stroke down to the baseline, making sure that it overlaps the end of the second stroke.

4 Stamp a few extra strokes to give the letter some weight.

capital height

baseline

Indicates an area that needs to be drawn in with a marker

SAFARI

Go wild! Whether your text is about a trip to the zoo, an African expedition, or a backyard adventure, these letters are easy to draw and fun to fill in. Zebras, tigers, and leopards all have interesting patterns that can be imitated to create adventurous-looking alphabets. Allow the shapes of the letters to influence the direction of the patterns. The letters can be adapted for captions, phrases, or titles in a range of sizes using the same tools.

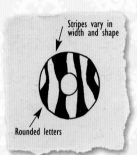

NOTE TO SCRAPBOOKERS Safari does not require a coordinating lowercase alphabet.

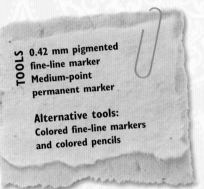

TOOLS
0.42 mm pigmented fine-line marker
Medium-point permanent marker

Alternative tools:
Colored fine-line markers and colored pencils

DISTINGUISHING FEATURES

These round letter shapes look overstuffed because they have small counter spaces, rounded corners, and no straight lines. They can be overlapped or drawn separately before adding animal markings. For a more realistic look, avoid stripes with straight sides and parallel lines. Maintaining fairly consistent letter heights and weights will help keep this alphabet legible.

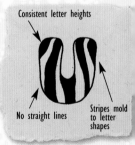

Stripes vary in width and shape

Rounded letters

LETTER-SPACING GUIDE

Letters overlap and bump into each other. Allow just enough space to make the words legible. See page 12 for more information on letter spacing.

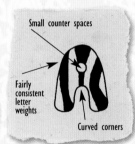

Small counter spaces

Fairly consistent letter weights

Curved corners

Consistent letter heights

No straight lines

Stripes mold to letter shapes

LETTER CONSTRUCTION: H

1 Outline the letter using a fine-line marker.

2 Outline the stripes. Notice that there are no parallel lines. Allow the letter shape to influence the stripes.

3 Carefully fill in alternate stripes using a medium-point marker.

VARIATIONS

Leopard spots

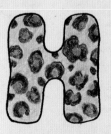

Tiger stripes

capital height

baseline

CLEOPATRA

These unique and unusual letters include shapes that are reminiscent of ancient Egypt. Serendipitously, they also look like the paper clips you might use to hold treasured travel memorabilia together until it can be added to a scrapbook. This alphabet is a pleasure to use and adds interest to pages about foreign lands and historical tours. Larger titles can be written using the same monoline tool, but a finer tool should be used for smaller text.

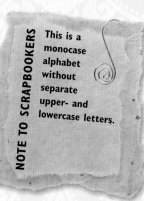

NOTE TO SCRAPBOOKERS This is a monocase alphabet without separate upper- and lowercase letters.

TOOLS
Medium-point permanent marker

Alternative tools: Any monoline writing tool

DISTINGUISHING FEATURES

This is a monocase alphabet created with a monoline tool, consisting of vertical letters constructed from simple geometric shapes. The triangular peaks and valleys used for some letters are reminiscent of the pyramids and are also found in Egyptian hieroglyphics. Other letters have trapezoid bowls that look like rectangular paper clips and are similar to the decorative elements found on the rims of ancient artifacts. There are no serifs on the letters, although V, W, X, and Y do have short horizontal entry and exit strokes. Some letters have very short ascenders or descenders.

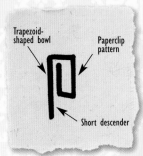

Trapezoid-shaped bowl

Paperclip pattern

Short descender

LETTER-SPACING GUIDE

Make some letters shorter and tuck them under the arms of diagonal letters (v, w, y). Descenders drop below the baseline. See page 12 for more information on letter spacing.

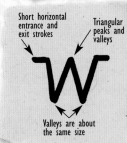

Monocase alphabet

Geometric shapes

Monoline letters

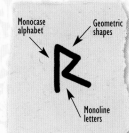

Short horizontal entrance and exit strokes

Triangular peaks and valleys

Valleys are about the same size

LETTER CONSTRUCTION: S

1 Draw the core shape without any pen lifts. Pause before each direction change.

2 Begin the second stroke above mid-height. Notice that there are no parallel lines.

3 Start the third stroke so that it overlaps the second and drops to just below mid-height.

LETTER CONSTRUCTION: A

1 Beginning at the top, draw the first stroke so that it slants slightly forward.

2 Start the second stroke so that it overlaps the first and ends below the baseline.

3 Add the crossbar so that it intersects the second stroke and overlaps the first at the baseline.

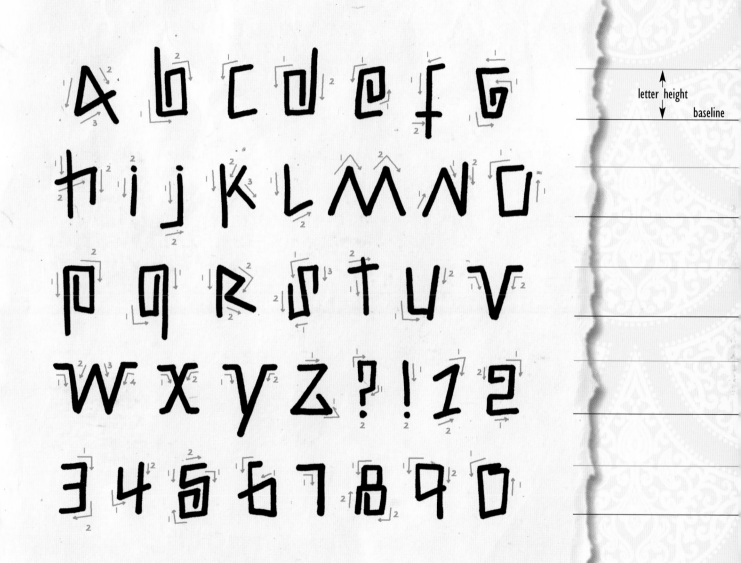

letter height
baseline

EASTERN BAZAAR

This alphabet's Asian flavor comes from the tapered strokes and the use of a brush marker. The letter strokes are created using pressure and quick release, which may require some practice. Intended for titles and captions only, this letter style is perfect for recording memories of once-in-a-lifetime vacations or for a special event featuring your favorite take-out food. Try fiber brushes in a variety of sizes for lettering at different heights.

NOTE TO SCRAPBOOKERS Eastern Bazaar does not require a coordinating lowercase alphabet.

TOOLS Pigmented fiber-tipped brush marker with ⅜-inch (10-mm) long tapered tip

Alternative tools: Pointed-brush pen

DISTINGUISHING FEATURES

Unusual letter shapes are constructed from a series of tapered strokes. These often end in slightly textured or wispy points that break through the guidelines. Letters have flat tops and often include short strokes that are made by releasing the pressure on the brush with a quick flick. This alphabet has a slight forward slant, but strokes within the same letter can have a slightly different tilt.

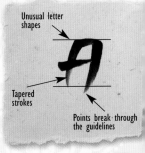

Unusual letter shapes

Tapered strokes

Points break through the guidelines

LETTER-SPACING GUIDE

The tips of the letters cut through the guidelines. See page 12 for more information on letter spacing.

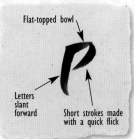

Flat-topped bowl

Letters slant forward

Short strokes made with a quick flick

Center stroke tapers to the left

Upward lift on bottom stroke

LETTER CONSTRUCTION: R

1 Position the brush marker as shown for each stroke. Apply pressure and then pull the first stroke downward. Note the stroke's slight curve and slant.

2 Apply pressure, then use a quick flick and release of pressure to taper the second stroke.

3 Begin the third stroke, quickly adding and then releasing pressure to taper it at both ends.

4 Apply pressure and then pull the fourth stroke downward, releasing the pressure gradually to taper the stroke.

LETTER CONSTRUCTION: Z

1 Position the brush marker as shown for each stroke. Apply pressure and then pull the first stroke to the right, releasing pressure to taper the stroke.

2 Apply pressure at the top of the second stroke. Begin to release the pressure about halfway through for a tapered stroke.

3 Apply pressure and use a quick motion for the final stroke, releasing pressure to taper it. Notice the slight upward slant.

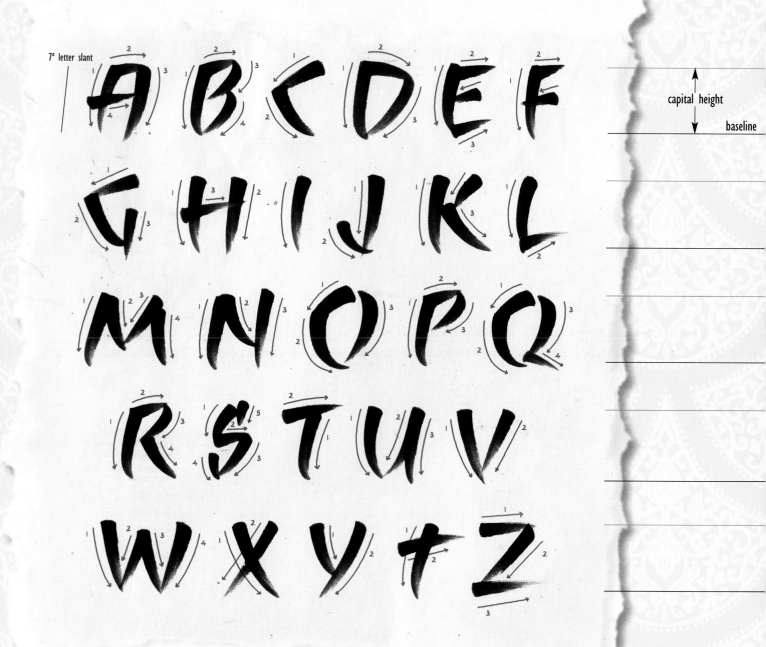

7° letter slant

capital height

baseline

STORE FRONT

You might find lettering like this in store windows or on signs announcing "Daily Specials" on your many travels. This is an excellent alphabet for captions or titles about the marvels of daytrippers and globetrotters alike. The tool used to create this alphabet may be a little unfamiliar, but with some practice it is fun to use. Pay careful attention to the start and finish of each stroke. Use a different-sized brush marker for larger or smaller lettering.

NOTE TO SCRAPBOOKERS Store Front is intended for titles and captions only. Use Miss Barrett (pages 86–87) at a smaller size for accompanying pieces of long text.

TOOLS Pigmented fiber-tipped brush marker with ½-inch (13-mm) long tapered tip

Alternative tools: Colored fiber-tipped brush markers

DISTINGUISHING FEATURES

This bold alphabet is written with a flexible fiber-tipped brush marker, which requires practice to master. The sans-serif letters are fairly consistent in weight, size, and shape, and a jaunty disposition is achieved by giving each stroke a slight curve. Bowls are forward-slanting oval shapes. A range of interlinear spacing is possible with this letter style, but it is most effective if lines of text are no more than one x-height apart.

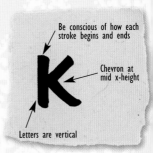

Be conscious of how each stroke begins and ends

Chevron at mid x-height

Letters are vertical

LETTER-SPACING GUIDE

All letters sit on the baseline. See page 12 for more information on letter spacing.

LOCVIR

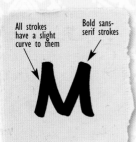

All strokes have a slight curve to them

Bold sans-serif strokes

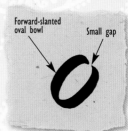

Forward-slanted oval bowl

Small gap

LETTER CONSTRUCTION: R

I Position the brush marker as shown. Apply pressure and then pull the brush downward in a vertical stroke.

2 Using the same brush angle, place the tip so that it overlaps the first stroke, then apply pressure before pulling the second stroke.

3 Position the brush as shown, then pull the third stroke so that it overlaps the second. Notice the slight curve.

LETTER CONSTRUCTION: M

I Position the brush marker as shown. Apply pressure and then pull the brush downward at a slight slant. Note that all the strokes have a slight curve.

2 Turning the brush slightly as shown, place the tip so that it overlaps the first stroke, then apply pressure before pulling the second stroke.

3 Repeat this process for the third stroke. Make sure that you come to a complete stop before lifting the brush.

4 Make the fourth stroke as before. Notice that alternate strokes have a similar slant.

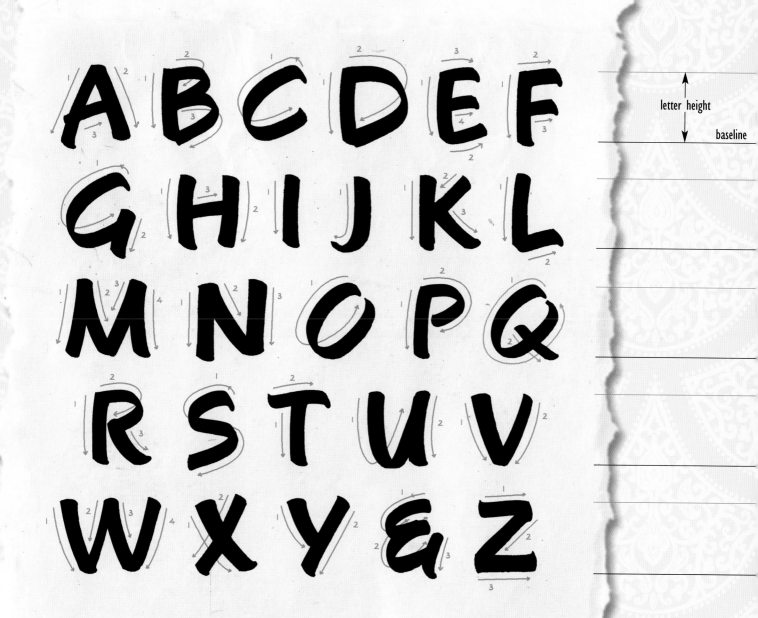

letter height

baseline

TROY

Inspired by ancient Greek symbols, this is an intriguing monocase alphabet that is fun to use. It is ideal for vacation stories about historical discoveries and ancient civilizations, or endless days on islands of boundless beauty. This letter style requires little practice and is created using everyday tools. It can be written at a wide variety of sizes using the same monoline tool, but a finer marker or pen should be used for very small lettering.

NOTE TO SCRAPBOOKERS This is a monocase alphabet without separate upper- and lowercase letters.

TOOLS Medium-point permanent marker

Alternative tools: Any monoline writing tool

DISTINGUISHING FEATURES

The many round letters give this alphabet its warm, encompassing feel, while the heavy influence of Greek symbols creates an exotic look. Unusual monoline letter shapes include a top-heavy S, while the C, G, M, N, U, and W shapes are based on the familiar omega symbol. Round letters have no vertical strokes but do have at least one horizontal terminal to give stability. There are no ascenders and only a few modest descenders, allowing a wide choice of interlinear spacing.

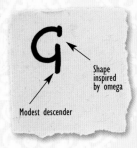

Shape inspired by omega

Modest descender

LETTER-SPACING GUIDE

All letters sit on the baseline. See page 12 for more information on letter spacing.

No ascenders

Heavily influenced by Greek symbols such as beta

Monoline letters

Curves break the guidelines

Unusual letter shapes

LETTER CONSTRUCTION: K

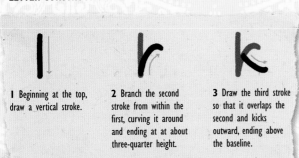

1 Beginning at the top, draw a vertical stroke.

2 Branch the second stroke from within the first, curving it around and ending at at about three-quarter height.

3 Draw the third stroke so that it overlaps the second and kicks outward, ending above the baseline.

NUMBER CONSTRUCTION: 8

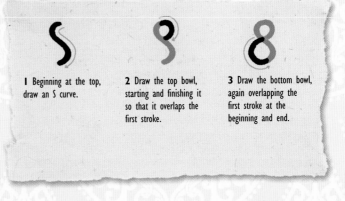

1 Beginning at the top, draw an S curve.

2 Draw the top bowl, starting and finishing it so that it overlaps the first stroke.

3 Draw the bottom bowl, again overlapping the first stroke at the beginning and end.

letter height
baseline

AREEBA

The decorated edges of the letters look hand embroidered to give this alphabet a Mexican flavor. Calligraphy markers are required, but since there are very few pen-angle changes, it is a simple alphabet to master. Areeba can be used for title pages and captions about Mariachi bands, trips to sunny Mexico, or a spicy mid-winter party at home. Changing the size of the calligraphy tools is required if you want to letter this style at a different size.

NOTE TO SCRAPBOOKERS Areeba does not require a coordinating lowercase alphabet.

TOOLS

5.0 mm pigmented calligraphy marker
2.0 mm pigmented calligraphy marker
0.50 mm pigmented fine-line marker

Alternative tools:
Traditional calligraphy dip pens or calligraphy fountain pens and a fine-line marker

DISTINGUISHING FEATURES

The bold letters are penned using only two basic pen angles, with the decorative edge using a third pen angle. The edge is added at a consistent distance from each letter, using a fine-line marker and a small-tipped calligraphy marker. The letters are dense, vertical, and do not have any serifs. They are uniform in size and weight and stand firmly on the baseline. Lines of text can be stacked closely together to create interesting texture.

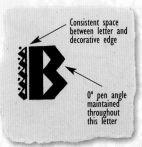

Consistent space between letter and decorative edge

0° pen angle maintained throughout this letter

LETTER-SPACING GUIDE

All letters sit on the baseline. See page 12 for more information on letter spacing.

"Embroidered" edge

All horizontals made with a 90° pen angle

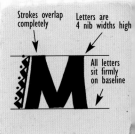

Strokes overlap completely

Letters are 4 nib widths high

All letters sit firmly on baseline

LETTER CONSTRUCTION: D

1 Using a broad calligraphy marker at a 0° (flat) pen angle, make a vertical stroke.

2 Maintain the flat pen angle for the second stroke. Note that the point of the chevron is just above center height.

3 Using a fine-line marker, add a line parallel to the first stroke.

4 Add the zigzag pattern using a smaller calligraphy marker at a 45° pen angle. Add the dots with the fine-line marker.

LETTER CONSTRUCTION: L

1 Using a broad calligraphy marker at a 0° (flat) pen angle, make a vertical stroke.

2 Turn the pen angle to 90° for the second stroke, which should overlap the first stroke.

3 Using a fine-line marker, add a line parallel to the first stroke.

4 Add the zigzag pattern using a smaller calligraphy marker at a 45° pen angle. Add the dots with the fine-line marker.

0° dominant pen angle (all other pen angles are indicated next to the stroke)

4 nib widths

capital height

baseline

MISS BARRETT

This tidy printing has both warmth and understated class. It is appropriate for a wide variety of occasions, and can be used to record either short phrases or long bodies of text neatly. The letter shapes were inspired by Italic (pages 104–105), but are upright and written with a simple monoline tool. Use a larger tool when writing at larger sizes in order to maintain the same visual letter weight.

NOTE TO SCRAPBOOKERS Adapt Italic Capitals (pages 106–107) to use as uppercase letters for Miss Barrett.

TOOLS
0.42 mm pigmented fine-line marker

Alternative tools:
Use any monoline writing tool in any color and size that suits your purpose.

DISTINGUISHING FEATURES

These monoline letters are low branching and have oval bowls that are very consistent in size and shape. The ascenders and descenders are slightly shorter than the x-height, and the letters are vertical and without serifs. The natural imperfections that occur when the human hand uses a fine tool give this alphabet a sympathetic nature, while a sense of subtle refinement is suggested by the tall, slender, oval shape that is echoed throughout this style.

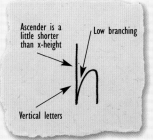

Ascender is a little shorter than x-height · Low branching · Vertical letters

LETTER-SPACING GUIDE

All letters sit on the baseline. See page 12 for more information on letter spacing.

iloevra

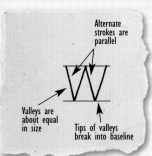

Alternate strokes are parallel · Valleys are about equal in size · Tips of valleys break into baseline

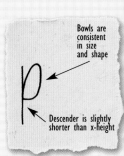

Bowls are consistent in size and shape · Descender is slightly shorter than x-height

LETTER CONSTRUCTION: A

1 Beginning at the top right corner, pull straight left before turning down and slightly left. End the stroke where it began.

2 Draw the second vertical stroke so that it overlaps the first and ends on the baseline.

LETTER CONSTRUCTION: M

1 Beginning at the top, draw a vertical stroke.

2 Briefly retrace the vertical before branching up and to the right.

3 Briefly retrace the second stroke before branching up and to the right. Notice that the counter spaces are about the same size.

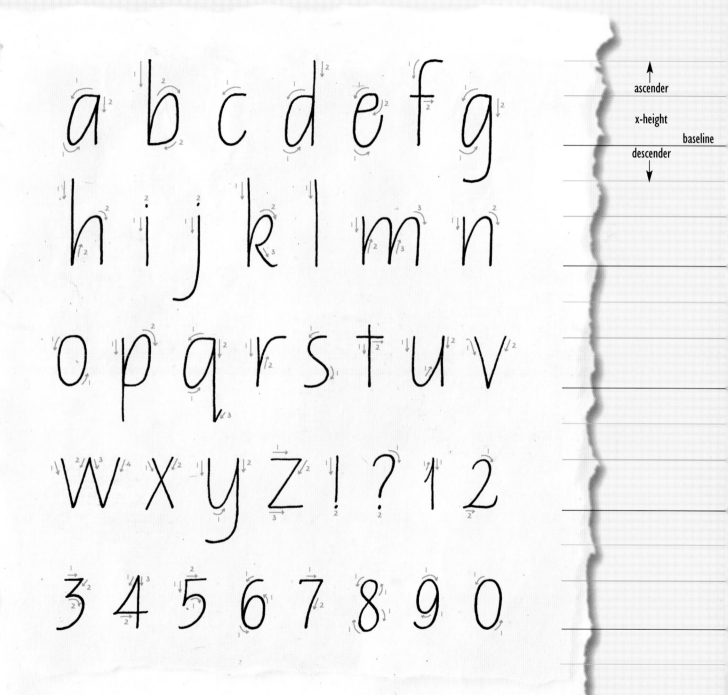

ascender
x-height
baseline
descender

RUDY

This simplified version of the typeface Neuland thunders with a feeling of strength and determination. Use it for titling, short phrases, or tightly packed blocks of text designed to leave an impression. Some practice may be required to master these letters because they are written using a calligraphic tool. Additionally, four of the letters require some pen manipulation. If you want to letter larger or smaller, use a different-sized calligraphic tool.

NOTE TO SCRAPBOOKERS Rudy does not require a coordinating lowercase alphabet.

TOOLS 5.0 mm pigmented calligraphy marker

Alternative tools: Traditional calligraphy dip pen or calligraphy fountain pen

DISTINGUISHING FEATURES

These stocky sans-serif letters are written with an x-height of 4 nib widths. All verticals are made with a flat 0° pen angle and all horizontals with a 90° pen angle. The rounded bowls on B, D, O, and Q require some pen manipulation; this means turning the handle of the pen clockwise while executing the stroke. The steadfast nature of this alphabet requires that the letters be very consistent in size and shape, and that all strokes land squarely on the baseline. Lines of text can be packed closely together to create a bold texture.

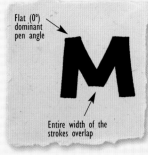

Flat (0°) dominant pen angle

Entire width of the strokes overlap

LETTER-SPACING GUIDE

All letters sit on the baseline. See page 12 for more information on letter spacing.

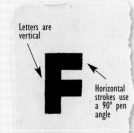

Letters are vertical

Horizontal strokes use a 90° pen angle

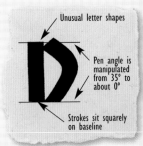

Unusual letter shapes

Pen angle is manipulated from 35° to about 0°

Strokes sit squarely on baseline

LETTER CONSTRUCTION: B

1 Beginning at the top, pull downward to create a vertical stroke using a flat (0°) pen angle.

2 Using a 35° pen angle, begin the second stroke with the left corner overlapping the first stroke and the right corner sitting above it. Curve the stroke to make a bowl that is about a third of the letter height.

3 For the bottom bowl, start with a 35° pen angle, then rotate the pen clockwise between your thumb and forefinger so that the stroke ends on a flat pen angle.

LETTER CONSTRUCTION: Q

1 Pull downward to the left and then the right to create the first stroke, maintaining a flat (0°) pen angle throughout.

2 For the second stroke of the bowl, start with a 35° pen angle, then rotate the pen clockwise between your thumb and forefinger so that the stroke ends on a 10° pen angle.

3 Using a 35° pen angle, pull a horizontal stroke that overlaps the bottom of the first two strokes and extends slightly beyond the elbow of the second stroke.

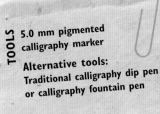

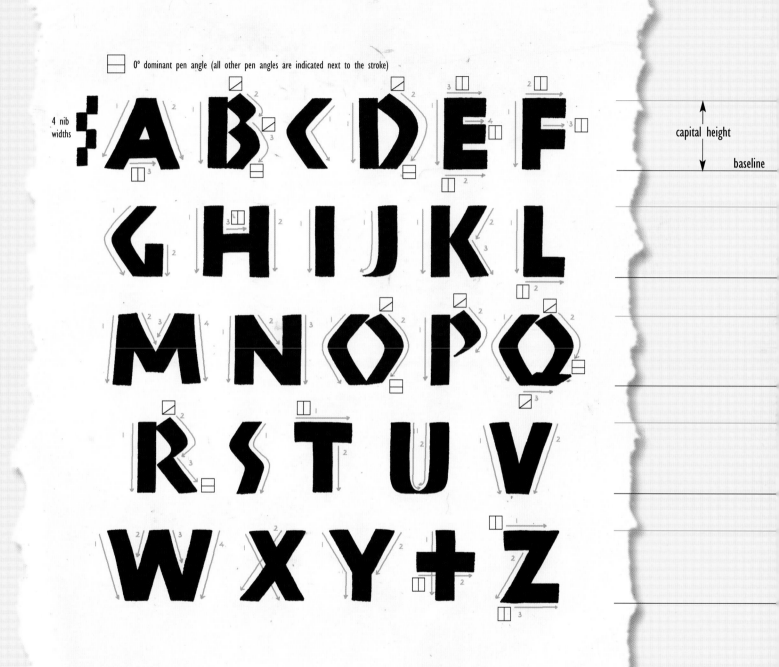

4 nib
widths

0° dominant pen angle (all other pen angles are indicated next to the stroke)

capital height

baseline

BRUSH EXPRESS

This lively and contemporary alphabet is great for high-energy title pages, and is especially appropriate for captions and phrases about teen parties and special events. The challenges of using a brush pen are well worth the effort, but special care should be taken to maintain fairly consistent letter weight within a project because minor changes in pressure will result in heavier- or lighter-weight letters. A range of letter sizes can be made with the same tool.

NOTE TO SCRAPBOOKERS Use Brush Express Capitals (pages 92–93) as the uppercase letters for this alphabet.

TOOLS

Pointed brush pen

Wet and dry brushwork: Experiment with the brush to see the range of letter sizes that can be made. This alphabet was drawn on rough paper with a fairly dry brush. A wet brush on smooth paper will result in letters with less texture. Brush pens come with black ink as well as a variety of colors, but permanence is a concern with some of these pens.

DISTINGUISHING FEATURES

These upright letters branch at mid x-height, and have ascenders and descenders that are slightly shorter than the x-height. They have angular bowls and somewhat narrow counter spaces. Contrasting thick and thin strokes are achieved by varying the pressure on the brush. Textured strokes are achieved by using a fairly dry brush on slightly rough paper. The texture adds to the dynamic appearance of this alphabet.

Ascender is slightly shorter than x-height

Mid x-height branching

Contrasting thick and thin strokes

LETTER-SPACING GUIDE

All letters sit on the baseline.

See page 12 for more information on letter spacing.

Narrow, angular counter space

Textured strokes

Descender is slightly shorter than x-height

LETTER CONSTRUCTION: S

1 Position the brush as shown and push to the left slightly before applying pressure on the downward stroke. Release the pressure and pull to the right to make a thin horizontal stroke. Apply pressure at the

top of the second curve, then release slowly to taper the stroke.

2 Turn the brush counterclockwise slightly and apply pressure before pulling downward in a curved stroke.

3 Begin the third stroke with the same brush angle and pressure as the second stroke. Release the pressure quickly to taper the stroke.

LETTER CONSTRUCTION: K

1 Position the brush as shown, apply pressure, and make a tall vertical stroke.

2 Turn the brush counterclockwise slightly. Begin with the tip of the brush to make a thin branching stroke. As you change direction on the bowl, apply pressure to broaden the stroke.

3 Turn the brush counterclockwise, apply pressure, and pull the third stroke diagonally. Release the pressure and flick upward at the end of the kick-leg stroke.

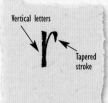

Vertical letters

Tapered stroke

a b c d e f g
h i j k l m n
o p q r s t u
v w x y z ? !
1 2 3 4 5 6 7 8 9 0

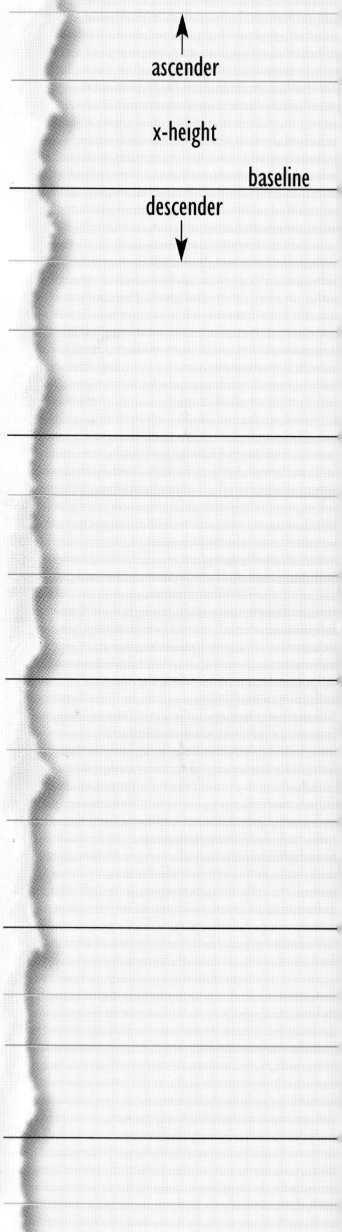

ascender
x-height
baseline
descender

BRUSH EXPRESS CAPITALS

This spirited and modern alphabet is designed for use with the lowercase Brush Express letters or can be used alone for titles. It is appropriate for catchy headlines, noteworthy events, and splashy title pages. Familiar letter shapes are given new life when made with a pointed brush pen. Although this tool may be challenging at first, a range of letter sizes and weights can be achieved by varying the amount of pressure applied to the brush.

NOTE TO SCRAPBOOKERS Use Brush Express (pages 90–91) as the lowercase letters and numbers for this alphabet.

TOOLS

Pointed brush pen

Alternative tools:
Experiment with the brush to see the range of letter sizes that can be made. This alphabet was drawn on rough paper with a fairly dry brush. A wet brush on smooth paper will result in letters with less texture. Brush pens come with black ink as well as a variety of colors, but permanence is a concern with some of these pens.

DISTINGUISHING FEATURES

These high-energy letters have verticals with a slight curve, horizontals that are not quite horizontal, and saucy brush flicks. Bowls that are either oval or angular and some hybrid shapes and widths contribute to the alphabet's contemporary feel. Contrasting thick and thin strokes are achieved by varying the pressure on the brush. This alphabet has an extreme textural quality due to the use of a moderately dry brush on a slightly rough surface.

LETTER-SPACING GUIDE

All letters sit on the baseline. See page 12 for more information on letter spacing.

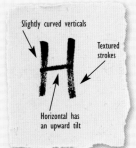

Slightly curved verticals

Textured strokes

Horizontal has an upward tilt

Oval bowl

Contrasting thick and thin strokes

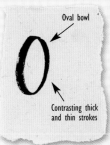

Angular bowl

Saucy brush flick

Hybrid letter shapes

LETTER CONSTRUCTION: M

1 Position the brush as shown. Apply moderate pressure to draw the first stroke. Note the slant of the stroke.

2 Turn the brush counterclockwise slightly and apply pressure before pulling diagonally. Note the slight curve of the stroke.

3 Turn the brush clockwise and apply a little pressure for the third stroke. This stroke is a lighter weight than the two previous strokes.

4 Maintain the same brush angle but apply more pressure for a heavierweight fourth stroke. Notice the slant of this stroke.

LETTER CONSTRUCTION: N

1 Position the brush as shown. Apply moderate pressure to draw the first vertical stroke.

2 Turn the brush counterclockwise slightly and apply pressure before pulling diagonally. Note that this is a heavierweight stroke.

3 Turn the brush clockwise and apply a little pressure for the third stroke. Notice that the stroke weight is similar to that of the first stroke.

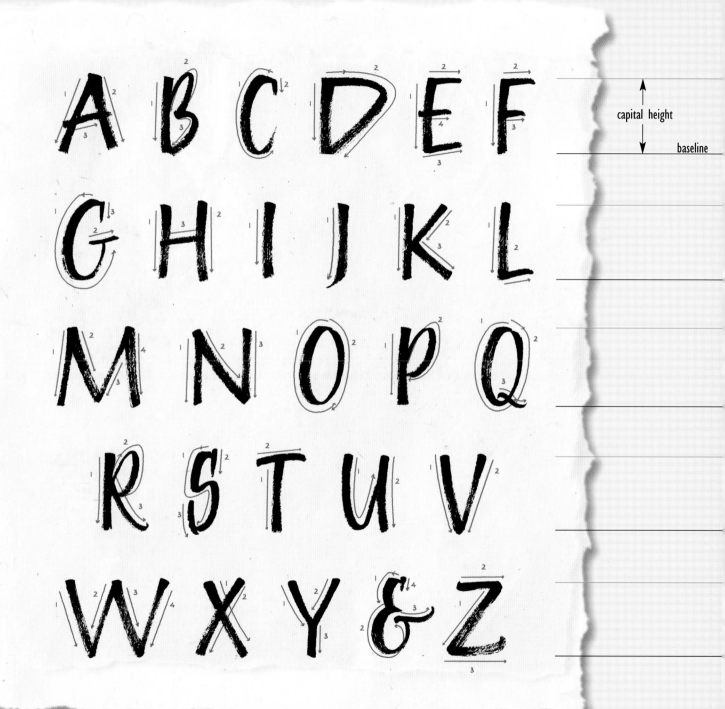

capital height

baseline

THORNTON

This confident and unique alphabet has a slightly quirky character that is ideal whenever bold statements or unusual captions are appropriate. A wonderful texture emerges when this letter style is used in a tightly woven text block. The alphabet is written with a broad-edged tool, so you should work slowly and always be aware of your pen angle. If you would like to create smaller or larger letters, change the size of the writing tool.

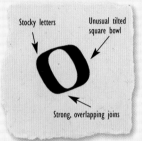

NOTE TO SCRAPBOOKERS
Thornton does not require a coordinating lowercase alphabet.

TOOLS
5.0 mm pigmented calligraphy marker

Alternative tools:
Calligraphy fountain pen

DISTINGUISHING FEATURES

This alphabet is built with rather unusual tilted square-shaped bowls. Letters are upright and stocky, written with an x-height equal to 4 nib widths. Short, pointed serifs are found at the tops and bottoms of the vertical strokes, and open letters have a manipulated "tooth" serif. Thornton has no ascenders or descenders, so lines of text can be stacked quite closely together to create a bold and interesting texture.

Stocky letters

Unusual tilted square bowl

Strong, overlapping joins

LETTER-SPACING GUIDE

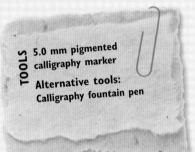

All letters sit on the baseline. See page 12 for more information on letter spacing.

Straight, erect verticals

Bowl is wider at the bottom

Short, pointed serifs

Manipulated "tooth" serif

Upper counter space is larger than lower one

LETTER CONSTRUCTION: B

1 Using a 20° pen angle, make a short serif at the beginning of the vertical. Continue around the bottom curve, ending when the stroke becomes thin.

2 Begin the second stroke inside the first. Pull slightly right and down for about a third of the x-height, then pull left for a thin exit stroke.

3 Start the third stroke so that it overlaps the second. Pull slightly right and down for the remaining two-thirds of the x-height, then pull left for a thin exit stroke that overlaps the thin end of the first stroke.

LETTER CONSTRUCTION: S

1 Using a 20° pen angle, pull the marker to form the S curve. Note that the upper curve is larger than the lower curve.

2 Start the second stroke so that it overlaps the first, then pull the stroke until it overhangs the bottom curve. Rotate the pen angle to almost 90° during the last half of the stroke to create a "tooth" serif.

3 Begin with the left corner of the nib at about the same height as the end of the first stroke. Finish with a thin exit stroke that overlaps the thin end of the first stroke for a strong join.

20° dominant pen angle (all other pen angles are indicated next to the stroke)

4 nib
widths

capital height

baseline

LYRIS

This is a kind-spirited alphabet with gentle nobility. Its character comes from a mixture of upper- and lowercase letter forms, most tall and thin but some wide, adding interesting texture to a body of text. It is appropriate for titles and captions, but also works for longer bodies of text, and is perfect for descriptions of ski trips, humorous captions, or sweet poetry. Try fiber-tipped brushes in a variety of sizes for lettering at different heights.

NOTE TO SCRAPBOOKERS This is a monocase alphabet without separate upper- and lowercase letters.

TOOLS Fiber-tipped brush marker with ⅜-inch (10-mm) long tapered tip

Alternative tools: Any monoline writing tool

DISTINGUISHING FEATURES

Tall, thin letters with a sprinkling of wide letters give this alphabet a lovely texture when used in larger blocks of text. The alphabet includes a mixture of sans-serif upper- and lowercase letters, including alternative forms of the letters e, n, and t. Some letters have very high crossbars, while others have very low ones. The brush marker allows you to add extra interest by introducing some modest contrast of thick and thin strokes. The letters are relaxed a little by adding a slight curve to most vertical strokes.

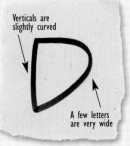

Verticals are slightly curved

A few letters are very wide

LETTER-SPACING GUIDE

All letters sit on the baseline. See page 12 for more information on letter spacing.

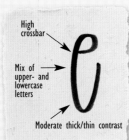

High crossbar

Mix of upper- and lowercase letters

Moderate thick/thin contrast

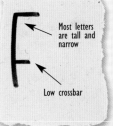

Most letters are tall and narrow

Low crossbar

LETTER CONSTRUCTION: Y

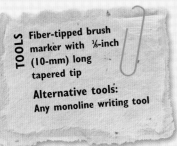

1 Position the brush marker as shown. Apply pressure and then pull a slightly curved diagonal that extends about two-thirds of the letter height.

2 Position the brush marker as shown. Apply pressure and then pull a slightly curved second stroke, ending so that it overlaps the first stroke.

3 Position the brush marker and apply pressure before pulling a short vertical stroke.

LETTER CONSTRUCTION: N

1 Position the brush marker as shown. Apply some pressure, then pull the first vertical stroke.

2 Retrace the top portion of the first stroke before moving right and down, applying more pressure for a heavier stroke. It should be curved and end above the baseline.

3 Position the brush marker and apply some pressure for the third stroke, which should cross the second stroke and end at the baseline.

letter height

baseline

UTOPIA

This alphabet is perfect for title pages and short captions about everyday fun and life's warm moments. Utopia is a monocase alphabet, so there is no need to learn both upper- and lowercase letters. Although the use of a pointed brush pen makes this letter style more challenging, a range of letter sizes can be made with the same tool. Try to maintain a fairly consistent letter weight within a body of text when using this tool, because minor changes in pressure will result in heavier- or lighter-weight letters.

NOTE TO SCRAPBOOKERS This is a monocase alphabet without separate upper- and lowercase letters.

TOOLS Pointed brush pen

Alternative tools: Experiment with the brush to see what range of letter sizes it can make. Once the pointed brush is mastered, these letters can be drawn fairly quickly, giving them a more spontaneous look. Brush pens come with black ink as well as a variety of colors, but permanence is a concern with some of these pens.

DISTINGUISHING FEATURES

Low-branching letters have rounded bowls that are slightly wider at the top than at the bottom. This shape allows the letters to be quite closely packed together, often touching one another at their widest points. Some letters have a short horizontal lead-in stroke or foot to give them more stability. The alphabet has short ascenders and descenders, allowing the use of less space between lines of text. A lovely mix of upper- and lowercase letter forms gives this style a warm and friendly feel.

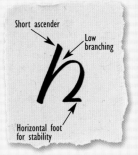

Short ascender
Low branching
Horizontal foot for stability

Rounded counter space is narrower at the bottom
Short descender

LETTER-SPACING GUIDE

LOCVIR

All letters sit on the baseline.

See page 12 for more information on letter spacing.

LETTER CONSTRUCTION: W

1 Position the brush as shown and apply pressure to produce a broad vertical stroke.

2 Turn the brush clockwise and apply less pressure for a narrower second stroke.

3 Apply more pressure to begin a broader third stroke. Release the pressure as you move around the curve, then increase it as you go up.

4 Turn the brush perpendicular to the baseline, apply some pressure, and add a short, horizontal serif.

LETTER CONSTRUCTION: K

1 Position the brush as shown and apply pressure to pull a broad stroke.

2 Begin with the tip of the brush to make a very thin branching stroke. As you change direction, apply more pressure to broaden the stroke.

3 Turn the brush as shown and add pressure to begin the third stroke. Release the pressure gradually to taper the leg as it kicks out.

Serif created with brush tip
20° letter slant
Compressed Uncial-like shape

20° letter
slant

letter height

baseline

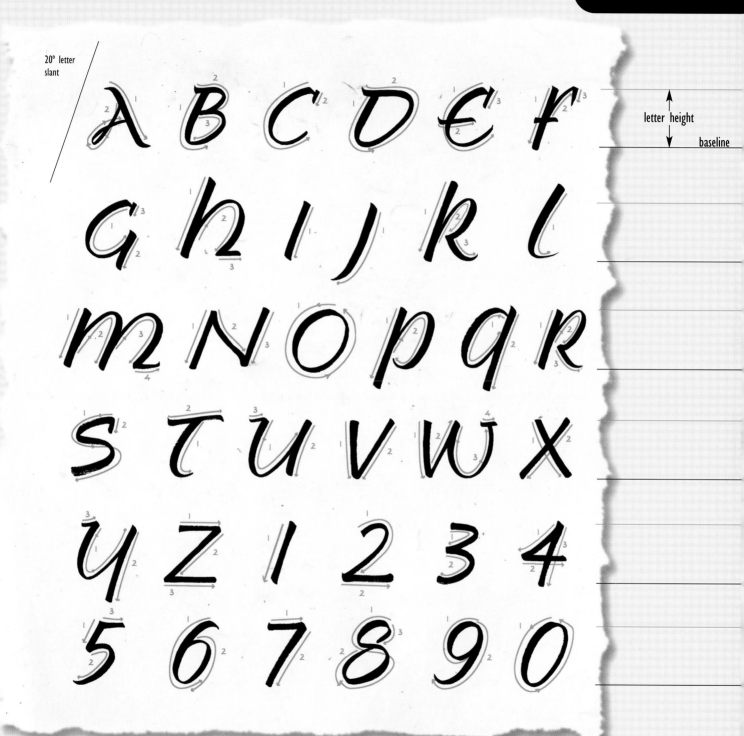

THICK 'N' THIN

The contrast of thick and thin lines made with a double-ended marker gives this alphabet a carefree feel. Thick 'n' Thin can be used for titles, captions, or longer bodies of text in a range of letter sizes using the same colorful tools. These letters are written fairly carefully, but can be done quite quickly. They work well for recording childhood firsts or those memorable moments when kids are captivated by their toys or bond with new friends.

NOTE TO SCRAPBOOKERS Use Thick 'n' Thin Capitals (pages 102–103) as the uppercase letters for this alphabet.

TOOLS Double-ended pigmented markers in various colors

Alternative tools: 0.50 mm pigmented fine-line marker and a medium-point permanent marker

DISTINGUISHING FEATURES

The thin end of the marker is used for bowls and serifs, and the thick end for stronger verticals. Single-stroke letters such as i, l, o, s, and t, and some numbers can be made either thick or thin to add interest and texture to your writing. This alphabet has ascenders and descenders equal in length to the x-height, and letters are vertical but not rigid. Letter shapes are fairly consistent in size and shape, with oval bowls and arches.

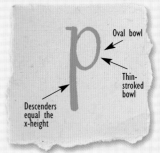

Oval bowl

Thin-stroked bowl

Descenders equal the x-height

LETTER-SPACING GUIDE

All letters sit on the baseline. See page 12 for more information on letter spacing.

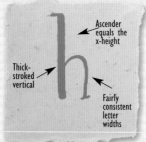

Ascender equals the x-height

Thick-stroked vertical

Fairly consistent letter widths

Fairly consistent letter shapes

Short, thin serifs

Slightly curved lines

LETTER CONSTRUCTION: M

1 Use the thick end of a double-ended marker for the first vertical.

2 Use the thin end of the marker for the second stroke, making sure that it overlaps the first one.

3 Still using the thin end of the marker, draw the third stroke so that it overlaps the second stroke and creates a counter space approximately equal to the first.

4 Use the thin end of the marker to add the serifs.

LETTER CONSTRUCTION: V

1 Use the thick end of a double-ended marker for the first diagonal.

2 Use the thin end of the marker for the second diagonal. Note the curve in this stroke.

3 Use the thin end of the marker to add the serifs.

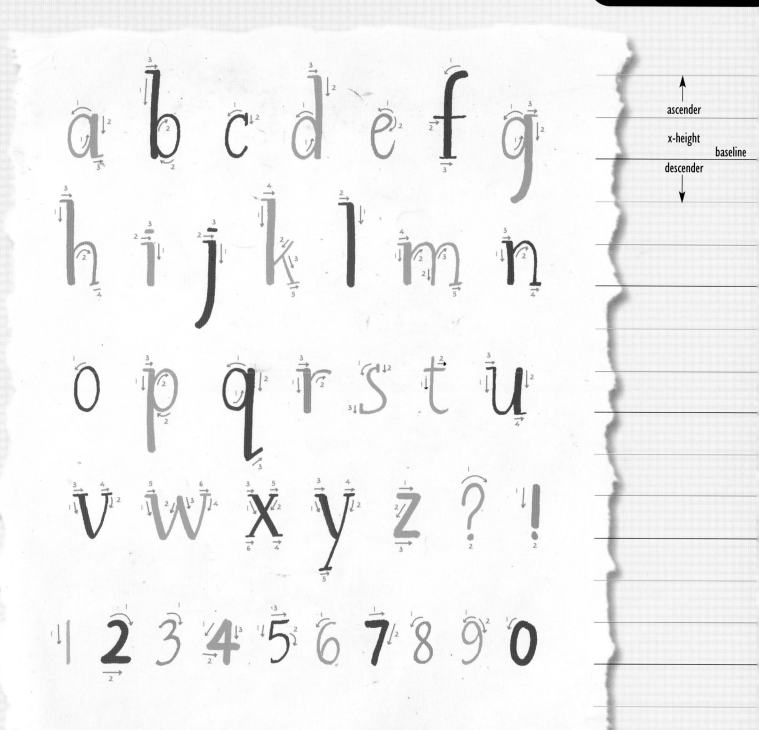

ascender

x-height

baseline

descender

THICK 'N' THIN CAPITALS

These uppercase letters are designed to be used with the corresponding lowercase alphabet, but are also rather appealing when used alone. This letter style can be used for amusing captions or clever titles about trial and error or life's challenges. A range of letter sizes can be made using the same tools. The letters can be bounced up and down or tilted backward and forward a little for an even more cheerful look.

NOTE TO SCRAPBOOKERS Use Thick 'n' Thin (pages 100–101) as the lowercase letters and numbers for this alphabet.

TOOLS Double-ended pigmented markers in various colors

Alternative tools: 0.50 mm pigmented fine-line marker and a medium-point permanent marker

DISTINGUISHING FEATURES

Double-stroked verticals provide interesting contrast with the thin-line bowls. There are very few absolutely straight lines in this alphabet—even the verticals have a slight curve to them. The letters are fairly narrow and have compressed oval bowls. Slender serifs provide stability for thin-line strokes and also extend across the tops and bottoms of verticals to connect thick and thin strokes.

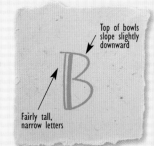

Top of bowls slope slightly downward

Fairly tall, narrow letters

LETTER-SPACING GUIDE

All letters sit on the baseline. See page 12 for more information on letter spacing.

LOCVIR

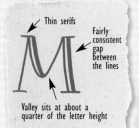

Thin serifs

Fairly consistent gap between the lines

Valley sits at about a quarter of the letter height

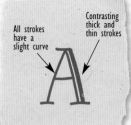

All strokes have a slight curve

Contrasting thick and thin strokes

LETTER CONSTRUCTION: M

1 Use the thin end of a double-ended marker for the first three strokes. Note the slant of the first downward stroke.

2 Draw the second stroke so that the valley sits at about a quarter of the letter height.

3 Splay the third stroke a little more than the first to leave room for a contrasting thick stroke.

4 Use the thick end of the marker to make a stroke parallel to the left side of the second stroke.

5 Use the thick end of the marker to add a stroke parallel to the third one.

6 Use the thin end of the marker to add serifs connecting the contrasting strokes.

capital height

baseline

ITALIC

This popular calligraphic letter style has a sophisticated appeal but remains easy to read. You can use this alphabet for any special occasion, but it is especially appropriate for graduations, weddings, and rites of passage. The letters are written with a broad-edged tool, so take special care that you work slowly and be aware of your pen angle. If you would like to create smaller or larger letters, you must change the size of your writing tool.

NOTE TO SCRAPBOOKERS Use Italic Capitals (pages 106–107) as the uppercase letters for this alphabet.

TOOLS
2.4 mm calligraphy fountain pen

Alternative tools: Broad-edged dip pen or calligraphy marker

DISTINGUISHING FEATURES

These letters have an x-height of 5 nib widths, a dominant pen angle of about 35°, and a forward letter slant of approximately 7°. The modest serifs and angular bowls are very consistent in size and shape, while the ascenders and descenders are slightly shorter than the x-height. The letter shapes are made with elegant thick and thin strokes that give this alphabet its "black-tie" look.

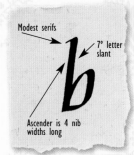

Modest serifs

7° letter slant

Ascender is 4 nib widths long

LETTER-SPACING GUIDE

All letters sit on the baseline. See page 12 for more information on letter spacing.

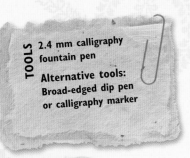

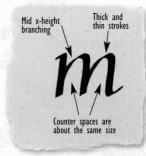

Mid x-height branching

Thick and thin strokes

Counter spaces are about the same size

Angular bowl

x-height is 5 nib widths high

Descender is 4 nib widths long

LETTER CONSTRUCTION: A

35° 35° 35°

1 Pull a short, thin stroke to begin. Maintain a consistent pen angle throughout the curve to achieve contrasting thick and thin strokes.

2 Start the second stroke so that it overlaps the first for a strong join. This stroke is fairly flat.

3 Pull the third stroke downward at a 7° slant, allowing it to overlap the first two strokes. Pull upward for a thin exit stroke.

LETTER CONSTRUCTION: S

35° 35° 35°

1 Begin and end the first stroke slightly inside the guidelines.

2 Start the second stroke so that it overlaps the first for a strong join. This stroke is fairly flat.

3 Begin with the right corner of the nib at about the same height as the end of the first stroke. Overlap the thin ends of these strokes for a strong join.

35° dominant pen angle (all other pen angles are indicated next to the stroke)

4 nib widths

5 nib widths

4 nib widths

7° letter slant

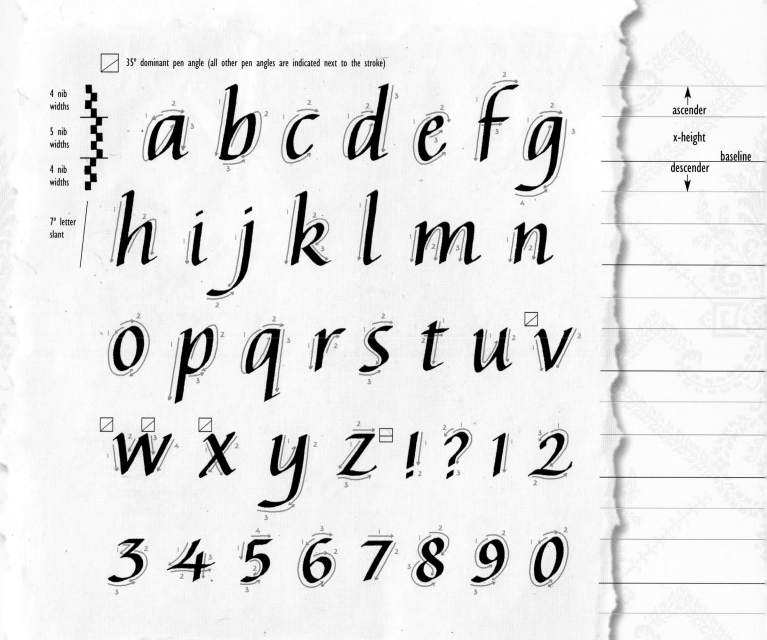

ascender

x-height

baseline

descender

ITALIC CAPITALS

This alphabet is designed to accompany the lowercase Italic letters, but can also be used on its own for titles or accent words. The calligraphic nature of this alphabet produces a refined look, making it appropriate for benchmark moments such as christenings, bar mitzvahs, or high school proms. Take special care that you work slowly and always be aware of your pen angle. Use a different-sized tool if you would like to create this alphabet at a different x-height.

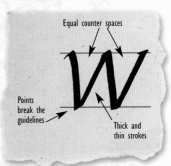

NOTE TO SCRAPBOOKERS Use Italic (pages 104–105) as the lowercase letters and numbers for this alphabet.

TOOLS 2.4 mm calligraphy fountain pen

Alternative tools: Broad-edged dip pen or calligraphy marker

DISTINGUISHING FEATURES

These letters are written at a height of 7 nib widths, with a dominant pen angle of approximately 25°, and a forward slant of about 7°. They have oval-shaped bowls and modest serifs. The broad-edged tool gives these letters their elegant thick and thin lines. Experienced calligraphers may wish to add a flourish to accent the first letter in a body of text. All letters sit on the baseline, but oval bowls and the points of diagonal strokes break the guidelines.

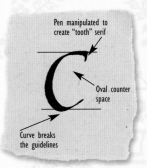

Pen manipulated to create "tooth" serif

Oval counter space

Curve breaks the guidelines

LETTER-SPACING GUIDE

LOCVIR

All letters sit on the baseline.

See page 12 for more information on letter spacing.

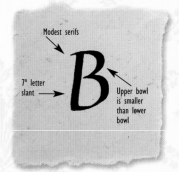

Modest serifs

7° letter slant

Upper bowl is smaller than lower bowl

LETTER CONSTRUCTION: B

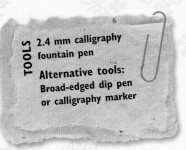

1 Begin with a serif, then complete the vertical stroke. Pause at the baseline, then pull right and slightly up until the stroke thins.

2 Start the second stroke so that it overlaps the first at the top and stops just above center height.

3 Start and end the third stroke so that it overlaps the thin ends of both the first and second strokes.

LETTER CONSTRUCTION: A

1 Pull the first stroke diagonally down to the left.

2 Start the second stroke so that it overlaps the first at the top. Release upward along the pen angle for a thin exit stroke.

3 Position the crossbar so that it overlaps both the first and second strokes. Notice that this stroke is tilted slightly upward.

Equal counter spaces

Points break the guidelines

Thick and thin strokes

25° dominant pen angle (all other pen angles are indicated next to the stroke)

7 nib widths

7° letter slant

capital height

baseline

ROMAN MAJUSCULES

These carefully constructed letters have similar proportions to those found on the Trajan Column in Rome. They can be used alone for titles of monumental importance, or in combination with the lowercase Roman Minuscules for captions and text. This letter style is quite conservative and appropriate for honoring life achievements. A different size of tool is required if you would like to letter this alphabet at a different height.

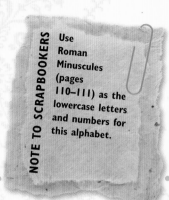

NOTE TO SCRAPBOOKERS Use Roman Minuscules (pages 110–111) as the lowercase letters and numbers for this alphabet.

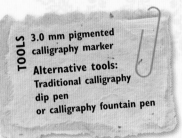

TOOLS 3.0 mm pigmented calligraphy marker

Alternative tools: Traditional calligraphy dip pen or calligraphy fountain pen

DISTINGUISHING FEATURES

These vertical letters with modest hooked serifs are written at a height of 7 nib widths and a dominant pen angle of 30°. Round bowls and the points of diagonal letters should break the guidelines, because otherwise these letters will look smaller than the others, even though in reality they would not be. Be conscious of pen angles and of how each stroke begins and ends. Relative letter widths are also intrinsic to the classic look of this alphabet.

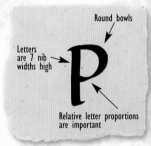

Round bowls

Letters are 7 nib widths high

Relative letter proportions are important

LETTER-SPACING GUIDE

All letters sit on the baseline. See page 12 for more information on letter spacing.

LOCVIR

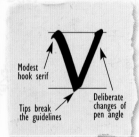

Modest hook serif

Tips break the guidelines

Deliberate changes of pen angle

30° dominant pen angle

Vertical letters

Chevron is at mid x-height

LETTER CONSTRUCTION: Y

1 Using a 45° pen angle, begin with a hook serif and then pull a diagonal stroke for about two-thirds of the letter height.

2 Changing to a pen angle of about 20°, begin with a small hooked serif and then pull the second diagonal stroke.

3 Use a pen angle of about 30° for the final vertical stroke. Finish this stroke with a hooked serif.

LETTER CONSTRUCTION: P

1 Using a pen angle of 30°, pull a vertical stroke with hooked serifs.

2 Using the same pen angle, start the second stroke so that it overlaps the first one and ends just below half the letter height.

3 Maintaining the same pen angle, complete the third stroke so that it overlaps the others and closes the bowl.

30° dominant pen angle (all other pen angles are indicated next to the stroke)

7 nib widths

capital height

baseline

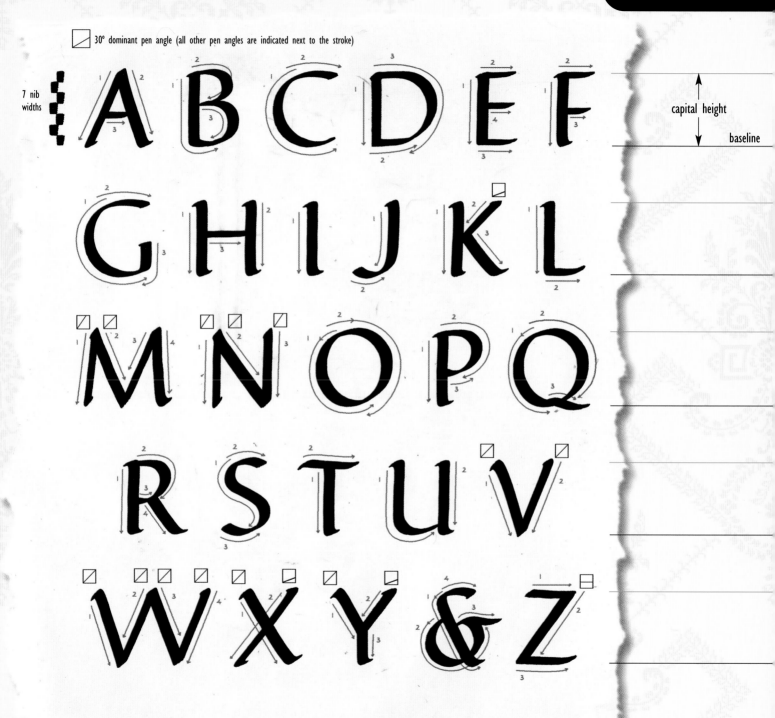

ROMAN MINUSCULES

Roman Minuscules is a variation of a standard calligraphic letter style. This round alphabet is practical, easy to read, and gives a formal look to long bodies of text. It is also fitting for captions, labels, or descriptions about formal occasions and noteworthy accomplishments. To achieve letters with the same proportions, you must use an appropriately sized calligraphic tool whenever this alphabet is penned at a different size.

NOTE TO SCRAPBOOKERS Use Roman Majuscules (pages 108–109) as the uppercase letters for this alphabet.

TOOLS
3.0 mm pigmented calligraphy marker

Alternative tools:
Traditional calligraphy dip pen
or calligraphy fountain pen

Distinguishing features

Classic thick and thin strokes are achieved by using a broad-edged lettering tool. Letters are vertical, have round bowls and arches, and modest hooked serifs. Ascenders and descenders are 2.5 nib widths and the x-height is 4.5 nib widths. Careful attention must be given to pen angles and letter construction to create this letter style.

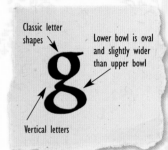

Classic letter shapes

Lower bowl is oval and slightly wider than upper bowl

Vertical letters

LETTER-SPACING GUIDE

All letters sit on the baseline. See page 12 for more information on letter spacing.

iloevra

x-height is 4.5 nib widths

Descender is 2.5 nib widths long

Round bowl

Ascender is 2.5 nib widths long

Round arch

Modest hook serifs

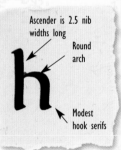

LETTER CONSTRUCTION: Z

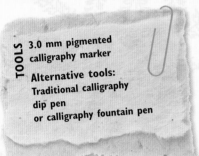

1 Using a pen angle of 30°, make a horizontal stroke from left to right.

2 Flatten the pen angle to about 0° for the diagonal stroke, allowing it to overlap the first stroke.

3 Steepen the pen angle back to 30° for the bottom horizontal, which should overlap the second stroke.

LETTER CONSTRUCTION: S

1 Beginning at the top, pull the first stroke downward using a 30° pen angle.

2 Maintain the same pen angle for the second stroke, which should be only slightly curved.

3 Using the same pen angle again, keep the third stroke subtly curved to ensure an open counter space.

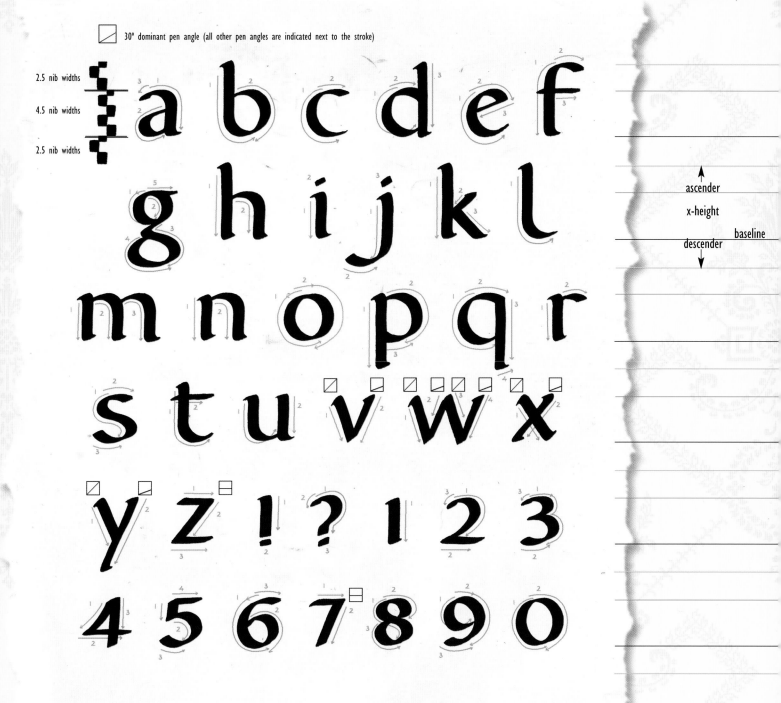

30° dominant pen angle (all other pen angles are indicated next to the stroke)

2.5 nib widths

4.5 nib widths

2.5 nib widths

a b c d e f
g h i j k l
m n o p q r
s t u v w x
y z ! ? 1 2 3
4 5 6 7 8 9 0

ascender
x-height
baseline
descender

DIANNAH

This calligraphic hybrid features the graceful branching of Italic (pages 104–105) and the round, open feel of Uncial (pages 114–115), giving character and warmth to this otherwise formal-looking letter style. This alphabet is appropriate for grand stories of loyal friendships and family histories, and can be used for titles, captions, and longer bodies of text. A different-sized calligraphic tip is required if you would like to write smaller or larger.

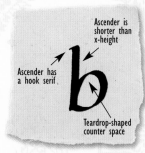

NOTE TO SCRAPBOOKERS: Adapt Roman Majuscules (pages 108–109) to use as uppercase letters for Diannah.

TOOLS
2.4 mm calligraphy fountain pen

Alternative tools:
Traditional broad-edged dip pen or calligraphy marker

DISTINGUISHING FEATURES

This is a calligraphic alphabet with a dominant pen angle of 25°, an x-height of 5 nib widths, and a slight forward slant of about 3°. Ascenders have modest hook serifs, while descenders have simple hairline serifs. Rounded bowls and mid x-height branching are combined to create teardrop-shaped bowls, while a traditional round o and c help relate this alphabet to the uppercase Roman Majuscules (pages 108–109).

Ascender is shorter than x-height

Ascender has a hook serif

Teardrop-shaped counter space

LETTER-SPACING GUIDE

Letters sit on the baseline and serifs break through it.

iloevra

See page 12 for more information on letter spacing.

Thick and thin contrast

Branching at mid x-height

Hairline serif

x-height equals 5 nib widths

Descender is shorter than x-height

3° letter slant

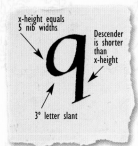

LETTER CONSTRUCTION: U

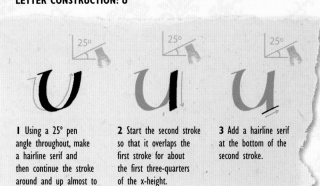

1 Using a 25° pen angle throughout, make a hairline serif and then continue the stroke around and up almost to the top of the x-height.

2 Start the second stroke so that it overlaps the first stroke for about the first three-quarters of the x-height.

3 Add a hairline serif at the bottom of the second stroke.

LETTER CONSTRUCTION: B

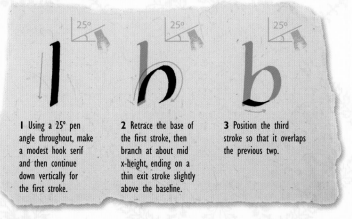

1 Using a 25° pen angle throughout, make a modest hook serif and then continue down vertically for the first stroke.

2 Retrace the base of the first stroke, then branch at about mid x-height, ending on a thin exit stroke slightly above the baseline.

3 Position the third stroke so that it overlaps the previous two.

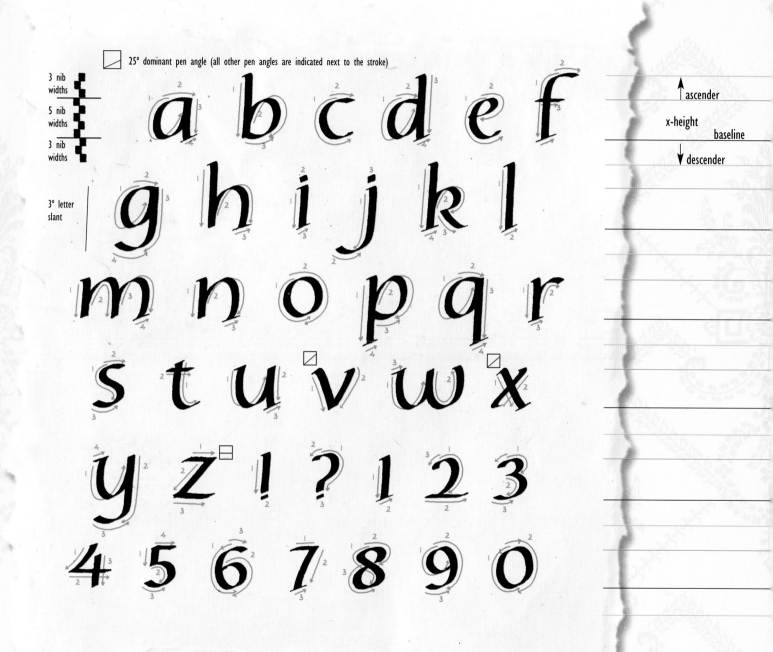

25° dominant pen angle (all other pen angles are indicated next to the stroke)

3 nib widths

5 nib widths

3 nib widths

3° letter slant

ascender

x-height

baseline

descender

UNCIAL

This sturdy calligraphic alphabet is full of warmth and character. It can be used for a wide range of events, but seems just right to follow a boy or girl from childhood adventures to youthful accomplishments. It is appropriate for titles and captions, but also creates a lovely texture when used in a text block. Try to work slowly and be aware of your pen angle. If you would like to create smaller or larger letters, change the size of the writing tool.

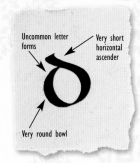

NOTE TO SCRAPBOOKERS This is a monocase alphabet without separate upper- and lowercase letters.

Uncommon letter forms

Very short horizontal ascender

Very round bowl

DISTINGUISHING FEATURES

This alphabet has strong, arching letters with large, round bowls and very simple, modest serifs. An interesting mix of upper- and lowercase letters as well as a few uncommon forms give Uncial a warm, friendly feel, while its calligraphic nature imbues it with a slightly more formal appeal. The alphabet has short ascenders and descenders, so less space is needed between lines of text.

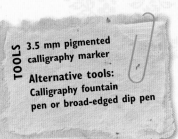

TOOLS 3.5 mm pigmented calligraphy marker

Alternative tools: Calligraphy fountain pen or broad-edged dip pen

Strong arch

Ascender is 2 nib widths long

Strong, sturdy letters

LETTER-SPACING GUIDE

Locvir

All letters sit on the baseline.

See page 12 for more information on letter spacing.

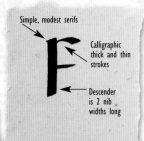

Simple, modest serifs

Calligraphic thick and thin strokes

Descender is 2 nib widths long

LETTER CONSTRUCTION: N

1 With a 55° pen angle, make a vertical stroke.

2 Flatten the pen angle to 40° and cup the second stroke slightly. Notice that the stroke stops above the baseline.

3 Steepen the pen angle to 55° again for the third stroke, and be sure to overlap the tip of the previous stroke.

LETTER CONSTRUCTION: W

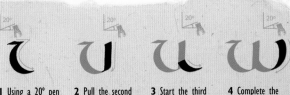

1 Using a 20° pen angle, pull a short horizontal serif. Pause before continuing around the counter space.

2 Pull the second stroke to the left at the bottom so that it overlaps the first stroke to ensure a strong join.

3 Start the third stroke so that it overlaps the second stroke.

4 Complete the fourth stroke so that the thin end overlaps the thin end of the third stroke to make a strong join.

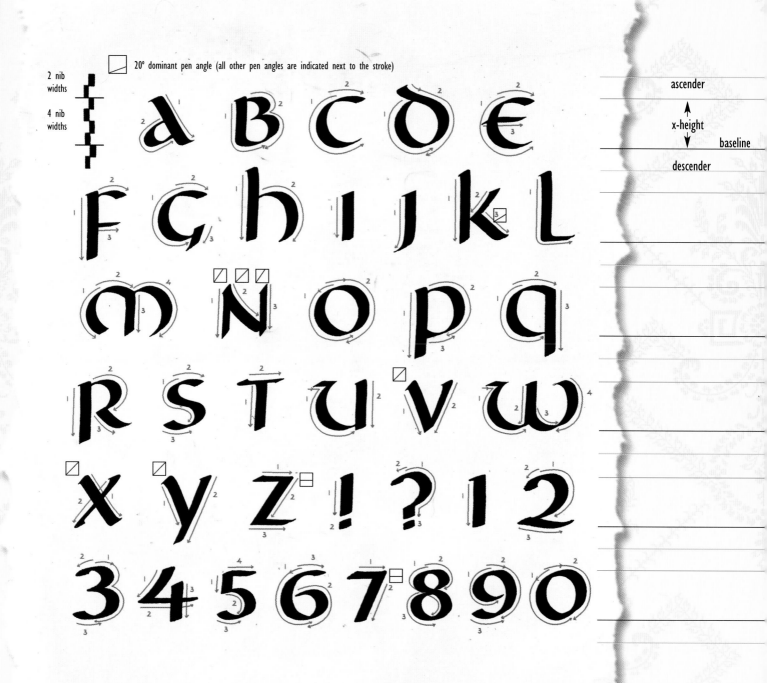

2 nib widths

4 nib widths

20° dominant pen angle (all other pen angles are indicated next to the stroke)

ascender

x-height

baseline

descender

SCHOOLBOOK

This familiar and legible alphabet is written with easy-to-handle tools. This style can be used for long text, simple captions, or lengthy quotes, and is just as appropriate for recording school memories as it is for sports events. To create larger letters, use a larger marker. This alphabet is also used as a basis for Morse Code (pages 46–47) and Flower Power (pages 54–55).

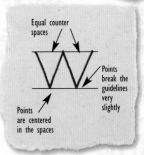

NOTE TO SCRAPBOOKERS Use Schoolbook Capitals (pages 118–119) as the uppercase letters for this alphabet.

TOOLS 0.50 mm pigmented fine-line marker

Alternative tools: Colored fine-line markers, colored pencils, or gel pens

DISTINGUISHING FEATURES

Schoolbook is a monoline alphabet based on traditional Roman minuscules. It is written slowly and methodically, but the tools and letter shapes are familiar. Vertical letters have strong arches and round bowls that are very consistent in size and shape. The ascenders and descenders for this letter style are the same length as the x-height.

Equal counter spaces

Points break the guidelines very slightly

Points are centered in the spaces

Strong arch

Descender is equal to x-height

Round bowl breaks the guidelines very slightly

LETTER-SPACING GUIDE

iloevra

All letters sit on the baseline.

See page 12 for more information on letter spacing.

LETTER CONSTRUCTION: G

1 Draw the first stroke of the small, round upper bowl, which should be about three-quarters of the x-height.

2 Complete the bowl so that the second stroke overlaps the first.

3 Start the third stroke so that it overlaps the others, creating a horizontal oval lower bowl that is wider than the upper bowl.

4 Pull the last stroke almost flat and along the top guideline. Keep it short.

LETTER CONSTRUCTION: M

1 Draw the first vertical stroke, beginning at the top.

2 Start the second stroke so that it overlaps the first. Keep the top round and the vertical drop straight.

3 Start the third stroke so that it overlaps the second, matching the size and shape of the first segment.

Round letter top

Ascender is equal to x-height

Letters are vertical and stable

ascender

x-height

baseline

descender

SCHOOLBOOK CAPITALS

Schoolbook Capitals is a standard alphabet with classic proportions. This style can be used alone for neat titles, captions, and banners, or as the uppercase letters to accompany the lowercase Schoolbook. This alphabet works well on scrapbook pages that require a lot of short phrases or labels. To create larger letters, use a larger marker. This alphabet is also used as a basis for Hairy (pages 60–61) and an uppercase Appliqué (pages 48–49).

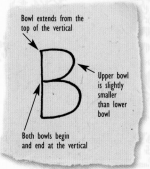

NOTE TO SCRAPBOOKERS Use Schoolbook (pages 116–117) as the lowercase letters and numbers for this alphabet.

TOOLS 0.50 mm pigmented fine-line marker

Alternative tools: Colored fine-line markers, colored pencils, or gel pens

DISTINGUISHING FEATURES

Schoolbook Capitals should be written slowly and carefully, but the tools are familiar and the letter shapes widely recognized. It is based on traditional Roman majuscules, with upright letters and very consistent round bowls. Take special care that you maintain the relative proportions of this alphabet's letters. These are not block letters; some letters are quite wide, while others are relatively narrow.

Bowl extends from the top of the vertical

Upper bowl is slightly smaller than lower bowl

Both bowls begin and end at the vertical

LETTER-SPACING GUIDE

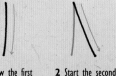

All letters sit on the baseline.

See page 12 for more information on letter spacing.

Points pierce the guidelines

Vertical letters with no slant

LETTER CONSTRUCTION: R

1 Begin at the top and draw a vertical stroke downward.

2 Draw the bowl a little larger than half the vertical stroke, allowing both ends to overlap the first stroke.

3 Start the third stroke so that it overlaps the second. Note the angle and placement.

LETTER CONSTRUCTION: M

1 Draw the first stroke with a very slight curve to the left.

2 Start the second stroke so that it overlaps the first, again curving it very slightly.

3 Start the third stroke so that it overlaps the second. This is also slightly curved.

4 Draw the final stroke with a slight curve outward.

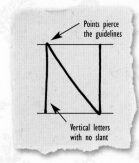

Open at top and bottom rather than curled in

Full, round counter space

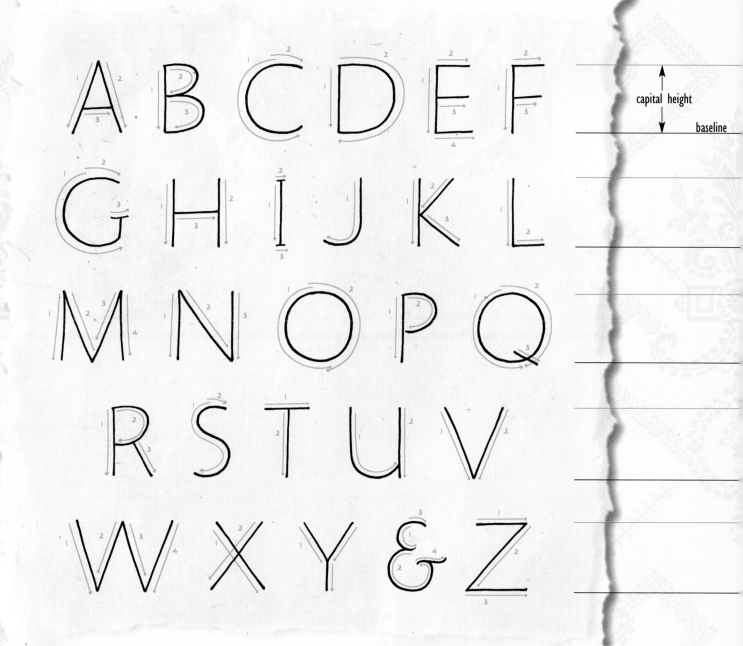

capital height

baseline

ACCENTS AND PUNCTUATION

This section features a variety of accents so that you can use the alphabets in this book to write words in different languages. There are also some common punctuation marks. Indicated next to each set of marks are the alphabets they are designed to be used with.

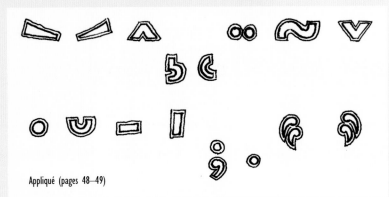

Appliqué (pages 48–49)

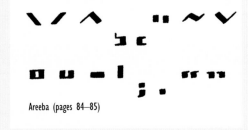

Areeba (pages 84–85)

Art Deco (pages 56–57), Art Nouveau (pages 28–29), Grandma's Handwriting (pages 32–33), Grandma's Handwriting Capitals (pages 34–35), Isabella (pages 22–23), Miss Barrett (pages 86–87), Morse Code (pages 46–47), Schoolbook (pages 116–117)

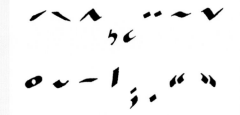

Ballerina (pages 20–21), Italic (pages 104–105), Italic Capitals (pages 106–107)

Art Deco Capitals (pages 58–59), Art Nouveau Capitals (pages 30–31), Hairy (pages 60–61), Isabella Capitals (pages 24–25), Once Upon a Time (pages 40–41), Pajama Stripes (pages 42–43), Safari (pages 74–75), Schoolbook Capitals (pages 118–119), Stick Letter Capitals (pages 72–73)

Beach Fun (pages 50–51)

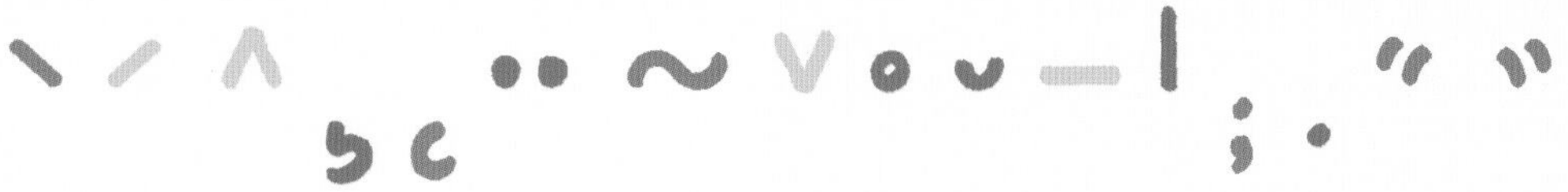

Beach Fun Capitals (pages 52–53)

Brush Express (pages 90–91), Brush Express Capitals (pages 92–93), Eastern Bazaar (pages 78–79)

Child's Play (pages 44–45)

Cleopatra (pages 76–77), Stick Letters (pages 70–71)

Curls (pages 62–63), Curl Capitals (pages 64–65)

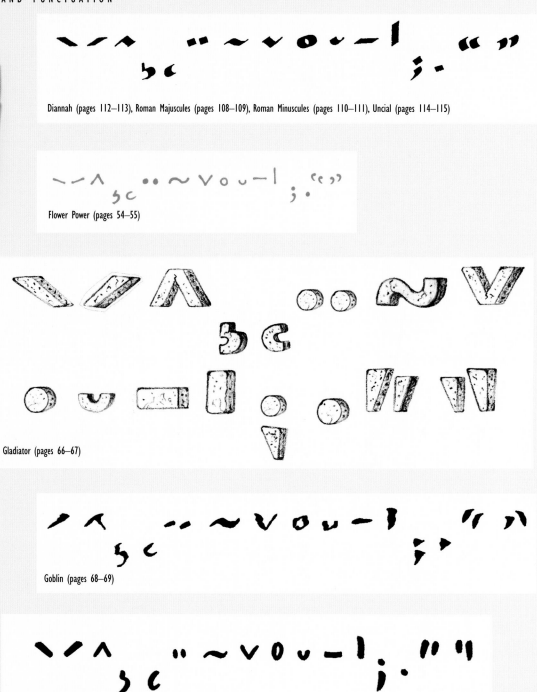

Diannah (pages 112–113), Roman Majuscules (pages 108–109), Roman Minuscules (pages 110–111), Uncial (pages 114–115)

Flower Power (pages 54–55)

Gladiator (pages 66–67)

Goblin (pages 68–69)

Lyris (pages 96–97)

Madeline (pages 36—37), Madeline Capitals (pages 38—39), Troy (pages 82—83)

Romeo (pages 26—27)

Rudy (pages 88—89), Thornton (pages 94—95)

Store Front (pages 80—81)

Thick 'n' Thin (pages 100—101)

Thick 'n' Thin Capitals (pages 102—103)

Utopia (pages 98—99)

GLOSSARY

Acidic Chemical term that indicates a pH value lower than 7.

Alkaline A pH value higher than 7; also known as basic.

Arch In a lowercase letter, the curved portion that attaches to the downstroke.

Ascender In a lowercase letter, the portion of the downstroke that extends above the x-height.

Baseline Writing line or guideline on which the letters sit.

Block letters An alphabet with letters that are all about the same width.

Bowl The strokes that form the enclosed area of a letter.

Branching stroke In a lowercase letter, the section that springs up and out from within the downstroke.

Broad-edged tool A tool having a writing tip with some width; calligraphy pen.

Calligraphic Refers to letter styles made with a broad-edged writing tool.

Capital height The height of an uppercase letter.

Counter space The partially or fully enclosed portion of a letter.

Descender In a lowercase letter, the portion of the downstroke that extends below the x-height.

Dominant pen angle The pen angle used most often for a particular alphabet (see also Pen angle).

Double stroke Two parallel strokes made with different-sized tools.

Downstroke A stroke made when the tool is moved from top to bottom.

Ductus The direction and order of the strokes that form a letter.

Entry stroke The first mark your pen makes when beginning a letter.

Exit stroke The last mark your pen makes when finishing a letter.

Flick A quick wrist motion; often used in brush lettering.

Flourish A decorative addition to a letter that extends beyond the letter shape.

Guidelines Temporary lines ruled to assist in making consistently sized letters in a straight line.

Hairline serif The thinnest entry or exit stroke a pen can make.

Hook serif An entry or exit stroke that looks as though it is cupping a portion of a very small circle.

Interlinear The space between lines of writing.

Kick-leg The lower diagonal stroke of K or R.

Letter slant The forward tilt of an alphabet. 0° is considered to be upright.

Lightfast Retains its original color when exposed to daylight over a period of time. Artist-quality materials are rated for lightfastness.

Lignin A component of plant cells that may contribute to the degradation of paper over time.

Lowercase Letters, often with ascenders and descenders, that are used to accompany capitals; also called minuscules.

Majuscules Uppercase or capital letters (A, B, C).

Minuscules Lowercase letters (a, b, c).

Monocase A complete alphabet that does not have separate upper and lower cases.

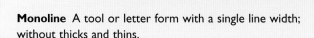

Monoline A tool or letter form with a single line width; without thicks and thins.

Mountain The highest points of an M.

Nib widths Used to determine the x-height, ascender, and descender of calligraphic alphabets.

Pen angle (flat, steepen) The angle of the broad-edged pen nib relative to the baseline. A flat pen angle (0°) is parallel to the baseline. As you rotate the pen counterclockwise, the pen angle steepens. A change in pen angle is sometimes necessary to make strokes of correct weight or thickness.

Pen manipulation While writing, the broad-edged pen is rotated between the thumb and forefinger in order to vary the width of the stroke.

Permanent Refers to waterproof writing fluid in a pen or marker.

pH neutral Neither acidic nor alkaline; having a pH value of 7 on a scale of 0–14.

Pigmented Refers to the quality of the color source used in writing fluid; usually means it is lightfast.

Pressure Deliberate stress applied to the writing tool and against the writing surface to make a thicker stroke.

Pressure–release–pressure A technique to make the beginning and end of a stroke heavier and the midsection of the same stroke lighter.

Retrace Go over the same line or stroke again with the writing tool.

Sans serif Without visible entry and exit strokes.

Serif An entry or exit stroke.

Shading In this book, strokes made thicker by filling in an outlined area. Traditionally, shading was added to pointed pen scripts, by adding pressure to a flexible pointed nib.

Stamp Leave an impression by pressing an inked object against the paper surface.

Stroke A section of a letter made without lifting the writing tool off the paper.

Thicks and thins Contrasting line widths within a letter; usually in reference to calligraphy.

Tooth serif A short, tapered, manipulated stroke that hangs down from the tops of letters C, E, F, G, and S.

Uppercase Capital or majuscule letters.

Upright 0° letter slant.

Valley The lowest points of a V or W.

Versals Decorative letters traditionally used in manuscripts at the beginning of chapters or paragraphs.

Verticals Downstrokes.

x-height The height of the body of a lowercase letter, excluding ascenders and descenders.

INDEX

Credits

Many thanks to my family and friends for their continued support. I am particularly grateful to Linda Prussick, Lynn Lefler, Cherryl Moote, and Carol Ayers for their ongoing encouragement, honesty, and inspiration, and especially to Lynn Lefler for generously sharing her expertise and giving me many kind nudges.

Quarto would also like to thank Anna Griffin Inc. (www.annagriffin.com) for the decorative background papers used in the Lettering Styles chapter.

All photographs and illustrations are the copyright of Quarto Publishing plc.

Resources

All of the tools used in this book should be readily available from your nearest arts and crafts store. In addition, below is a selection of websites where you can explore the options available. Many websites either allow you to order directly (and ship internationally) or list stores where their products are available.

www.7gypsies.com
www.annagriffin.com
www.benfranklinstores.com
www.bookmakerscatalog.com
www.colorbok.com
www.cornelisssen.com
www.craftsetc.com
www.currys.com
www.dickblick.com
www.gellyroll.com
www.hobbylobby.com
www.johnnealbooks.com
www.loomisartstore.com
www.luckysquirrel.com
www.makingmemories.com
www.michaels.com
www.paperinkarts.com
www.scrapbook.com
www.stampin.com
www.stampington.com
www.talasonline.com
www.uchida.com

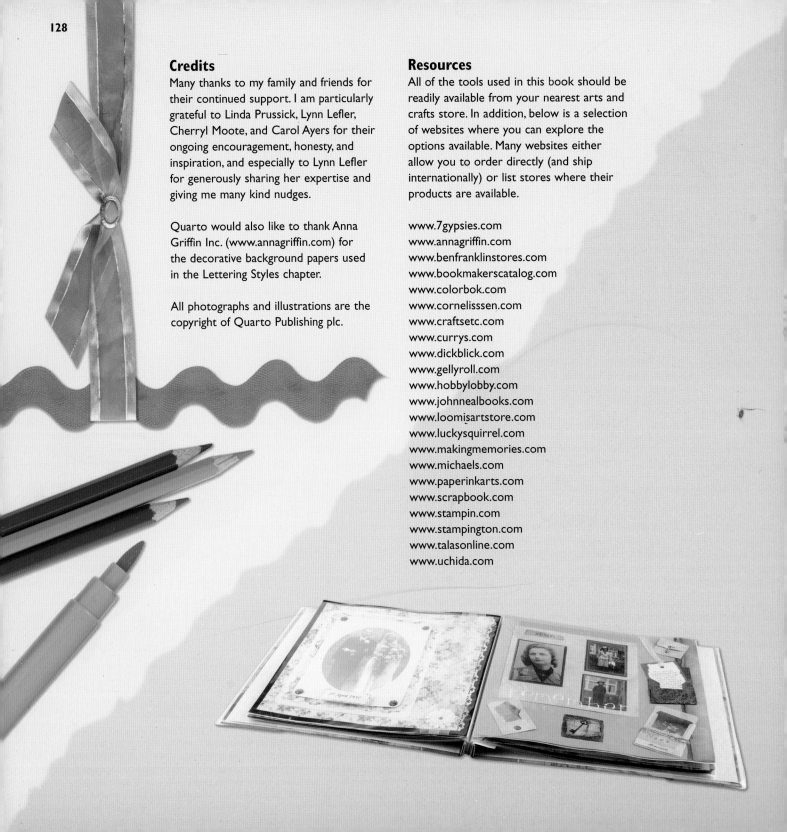